PANORAMA

BUILDING PERSPECTIVE THROUGH READING

3

KATHLEEN F. FLYNN
LATRICIA TRITES

with DENA DANIEL, ELLEN KISSLINGER,
RANDY POLLOCK,
and ANASTASSIA TZOYTZOYRAKOS

OXFORD
UNIVERSITY PRESS

OXFORD
UNIVERSITY PRESS

198 Madison Avenue
New York, NY 10016 USA

Great Clarendon Street, Oxford OX2 6DP UK

Oxford University Press is a department of the University of Oxford.
It furthers the University's objective of excellence in research, scholarship,
and education by publishing worldwide in

Oxford New York

Auckland Cape Town Dar es Salaam Hong Kong Karachi
Kuala Lumpur Madrid Melbourne Mexico City Nairobi
New Delhi Shanghai Taipei Toronto

With offices in

Argentina Austria Brazil Chile Czech Republic France Greece
Guatemala Hungary Italy Japan Poland Portugal Singapore
South Korea Switzerland Thailand Turkey Ukraine Vietnam

OXFORD and OXFORD ENGLISH are registered trademarks of
Oxford University Press

Developer: Angela M. Castro, English Language Trainers
Executive Publisher: Janet Aitchison
Editor: Phebe W. Szatmari
Art Director: Maj Hagsted
Senior Designer: Mia Gomez
Art Editor: Robin Fadool
Production Manager: Shanta Persaud
Production Controller: Eve Wong

ISBN-13: 978 0 19 430545 7
ISBN-10: 0 19 430545 7

10 9 8 7 6 5 4 3 2 1

Printed in Hong Kong.

Acknowledgments:

Cover art:
Hans Hofmann
Combinable Wall I and II
1961
Oil on canvas
Overall: 84-1/2 x 112-1/2 inches
University of California, Berkeley Art Museum; Gift of the artist.

The publisher would like to thank the following for their permission to
reproduce photographs: © Reuters/CORBIS, v (David Copperfield); Courtesy
Library of Congress, American Memory Collection, v (Harry Houdini); Chicago
Daily News negative collection, SDN-009529. Courtesy of the Chicago Historical
Society, 1; © Bettman/CORBIS, 2; © Bettman/CORBIS, 6; © Katie Diets/Index
Stock Imagery, Inc., 10; NASA, ESA, STSci, J. Hester and P. Scowen (Arizona
State University), 17; NASA/Hubble, 18; © Richard Cummins/SuperStock, 22;
STSci/NASA, 26; © Jonathan Elderfield/Getty Images, 33; © The Dorothea Lange
Collection, Oakland Museum of California, City of Oakland. Gift of Paul S.
Taylor., 34 (Dorothea Lange); Courtesy Library of Congress, Prints & Photographs
Division, FSA-OWI Collection, [LC-USF34-T01-009058-C], 34 (Migrant Mother);
Courtesy Library of Congress, Prints & Photographs Division, FSA-OWI Collection,
[LC-USF34-004090-E], 38; Photograph ID 523215: (Lewis Hine) "Workers
Stringing Beans" National Archives and Records Administration, Records of
the Department of Commerce and Labor, Children's Bureau, Record Group
102, 42; Courtesy William Arnett Collection, Atlanta, GA, 49; Matt Arnett,
2005, 50; © Walter Bibikow/Index Stock Imagery, Inc., 54 (Atlanta); © Stewart
Cohen/Index Stock Imagery, Inc., 54 (Charleston house); Photo of Finster's
cola bottle courtesy William Swislow/Interestingideas.com, 58; Woodshed
illustration, 65; © HVCB/Hawaii Tourism Japan, 66; © Joe Carini/Index Stock
Imagery, Inc., 70; © SCPhotos/Alamy, 74; © David R. Frazier Photolibrary, Inc./
Alamy, 81; © Bettmann/CORBIS, 82; © Visions of America, LLC/Alamy, 86; © Ken
Osburn/Index Stock Imagery, Inc., 90; © Bryan & Cherry Alexander Photography/
Alamy, 97; © Ewing Galloway/Index Stock Imagery, Inc., 98; Photo by Galen R.
Frysinger (www.galenfrysinger.com), 102; © Index Stock/Alamy, 106; © Visions
of America, LLC/Alamy, 113; © Ewing Galloway/Index Stock Imagery, Inc., 114
(Alexander Graham Bell); Courtesy Library of Congress, American Memory
Collection, [Digital ID: berlp 12040301], 114 (Bell's phone); © Dennis Hallinan/
Alamy, 115; Reproduced with Permission from Motorola, Inc. 122.

The authors and publisher would like to acknowledge the following individuals
for their invaluable input during the development of this series:
Russell Frank, Pasadena City College, CA; Virginia Heringer, Pasadena City
College, CA; Barbara Howard, Daly Community College, IL; Maydell Jenks, Katy
Independent School District, TX; JoShell Koliva, Newcomer School, Ontario; CA;
Kathy Krokar, Truman Community College, IL; Catherine Slawson, University
of California, Davis, CA; Laura Walsh, City College of San Francisco, CA; David
Caldwell, journalist

CONTENTS

TO THE TEACHER

Welcome to *Panorama 3*, a reading skills text for intermediate level students. *Panorama 3* combines high-interest reading passages from the content areas with a strong vocabulary strand and extensive reading skills practice to prepare students for the challenges of academic reading.

Each of the eight main units consists of three chapters, and each chapter has a thematically-linked reading passage. The first passage is about a person, the second about a related place, and the third about a related concept or event.

The book begins with an introductory unit, **Essential Reading Skills**, that presents and practices the core reading skills needed for academic success.

WHAT IS IN EACH UNIT?

Before You Read
This opening page introduces the theme of the unit. The questions and photographs can be used to activate students' prior knowledge and stimulate discussion before reading.

Prepare to Read
This section introduces the topic of the chapter. The questions and photographs encourage students to become engaged in the topic while sharing their own thoughts and experiences.

Word Focus
This matching activity introduces students to new or unfamiliar words that they will see in the reading passage. Students match the ten words with simple definitions.

Scan
This activity encourages students to make a prediction about a specific piece of information that appears in the passage. The aim is to motivate students to read the passages quickly as they try to find the answer.

Reading Passage
Each reading in Book 3 is about 1,000 words. The language is carefully graded using the Fry Readability Scale so that students gain confidence in reading; the average Fry Readability Score in *Panorama 3* is 7.0.

Check Your Comprehension
These multiple-choice questions check students' understanding of the passage. The questions include key skills such as understanding the main idea, reading for details, and reading for inference.

Vocabulary Review
This section reviews the vocabulary presented in the unit. It includes a wide variety of activities, such as **Words in Context** (filling in the gaps), **Which Meaning?** (choosing the definition that fits), **Wrong Word** (finding the word that doesn't fit the group), and **Word Families** (choosing the part of speech that fits). These activities help students use the new words as part of their active vocabulary.

Wrap It Up
This final section of the unit gives students the opportunity to discuss the theme of the unit with more confidence and holistic understanding. The last activity asks students to respond in writing about the passage they enjoyed the most. This activity reinforces what students have learned about the unit's theme.

The **Essential Reading Skills: Answer Key and Explanations** and a **Vocabulary Index** can be found at the back of the book for easy reference.

An *Answer Key* and *Assessment CD-ROM with ExamView® Test Generator* are available for use with *Panorama 3*.

Essential Reading Skills

David Copperfield, 1956–

Harry Houdini, 1874–1926

PREVIEW AND PREDICT

Before you read, **preview** and **predict**. When you **preview**, you look at the photographs and the parts of a passage. When you **predict**, you make logical guesses about content.

A. Look at the photographs only. (Don't read the captions yet.) Answer these questions.

1. Describe what you see. _____

_____

2. Do you recognize the men in the photographs? _____

3. Is the photograph on the right a new photo or an old one? How do you know? _____

4. What things can you guess, or **predict**, about the passage from the photographs? _____

B. Now read the captions. Answer these questions.

1. What information do these captions tell you? _____

_____

2. Are these men still living? How do you know? _____

_____

✔ Look at page 129 for the explanations.

C. Preview the passage on pages vii–ix. Read only the parts noted below. Answer these questions.

1. Read the title. Is the passage about a person, a place, or a thing?

   _____

2. What is the connection between the title and the photographs?

   _____

   _____

3. Read the subtitles. What is the purpose of the subtitles? _____

   _____

4. Which paragraph is the introduction? Read only the introduction.

   _____

5. Which paragraph is the conclusion. Read only the conclusion.

   _____

6. What do you **predict** the passage will be about? _____

   _____

D. Look for words with special markings. Answer these questions.

1. Find the words in **boldface**. Why do you think these words are in boldface? _____

2. Find the words in *italics*. Why do you think these words are in italics?

   _____

✔ Look at page 129 for the explanations.

WHAT TO DO WHILE YOU READ

SKIMMING AND SCANNING

Sometimes, you need to read quickly to look for certain information. This is called **skimming** and **scanning**. You **skim** when you read quickly. As you **skim**, your eyes **scan** for specific information. Use the passage and these questions to practice.

A. To skim, let your eyes move quickly over the passage. Answer these questions.

1. Is the passage fiction or nonfiction? How do you know? _____

   _____

2. What is the name of the third trick? _____

   _____

B. Before you scan, decide what to look for. Find each of these.

1. a five-letter **boldface** word _____

2. the name of a newspaper in *italics* _____

3. the date Houdini was born _____

4. the number of cups used in the cups and balls trick _____

5. the name of an ancient place _____

6. the name of Houdini's wife _____

7. an animal _____

✔ Look at page 129 for the explanations.

C. Now answer this question.

Guess if this is true or false. Circle *a* or *b*.

Siegfried and Roy made an elephant disappear.

a. True   **b.** False

Scan the passage quickly to check your answer.

✔ Look at page 129 for the explanation.

Magic Tricks and Illusions

For thousands of years, **magicians** have entertained people with **tricks** and **illusions**. Even beginning magicians can perform simple tricks with small objects and cards. Master illusionists like David Copperfield can make the Statue of Liberty in New York City disappear.

5   Let us examine some tricks and how both the magician and the **audience** play their parts.

Cups and Balls Trick

The cups and balls trick has been around for a long time. A painting suggests that this trick dates as far back as ancient Egypt 3,000 years ago.
10 The trick involves three cups and three small balls. The magician can make the balls pass through the bottoms of the cups, move from cup to cup, and disappear from one cup and appear in another place.

For this trick, the performer must have very quick hands. The magician gets the audience to look away from the real movement of the ball.
15 Beginning magicians often perform this trick.

Card Tricks

Many **amateur** magicians perform "find-the-card" tricks. The magician asks a person to pick any card from a deck of cards, without showing

continued

the card to the magician. Then the deck is shuffled, or mixed, and the
20 magician must find the original card.

This trick is actually very simple. Before shuffling the cards, the magician
casually turns the cards over and looks at the card that the person chose.

Cut and Restore Rope Trick

For this trick, the magician cuts a piece of rope, ties it together, and then
25 magically puts the rope back together in one piece. At least, that is what
the magician wants the audience to think.

The magician cuts the rope and shows the audience. This rope actually
does get cut. In reality, the magician loops another rope in the **palm** of
his or her hand and shows two additional rope ends. This gives the illusion
30 that the magician is holding two separate pieces of rope.

Houdini's Handcuff Escape

This trick uses handcuffs, the metal device that police use to hold a prisoner's
hands. To remove handcuffs, you need a key, unless you are a magician.

This trick was the specialty of Harry Houdini, who could escape
35 from multiple handcuffs and locks and chains, often under water. The
Great Houdini, who lived from 1874–1926, is perhaps the most famous
illusionist and escape artist of all time. He was just nine years old when he
began his career flying through the air on a trapeze in a local circus. At the
circus, his interest in magic tricks began. Houdini was an excellent athlete.
40 He was strong and could hold his breath under water for a long time. He
performed dangerous escapes that no one has been able to match.

Houdini's fame grew as he performed around the United States and
later in Europe. He met with the police in each city and usually had their
help when his acts opened in local theaters. But it wasn't just a matter
45 of having help. The newspaper, *The London Mirror,* had a set of special
handcuffs made. Houdini was still able to escape from them, and the
crowd in the theater went wild. Houdini became even more famous as a
result of this trick and the **publicity** that *The London Mirror* gave him. The
newspaper published many stories about the handcuff escape. Several of
50 his dangerous **stunts** are on film, and there are movies about his life.

Most of the time, Houdini used a hidden key. Houdini was able to
manipulate the key with his hands and even with his teeth. Houdini also
knew many tricks for opening handcuffs without keys. He could open
handcuffs with a shoestring or by banging them against a hard surface such
55 as a plate. He often kept a metal plate under his pants for that purpose.

Houdini's Metamorphosis Trick

Houdini was also famous for the Metamorphosis Trick. The word
metamorphosis means "a change." Houdini locked his assistant, usually his
wife Bess, inside a large trunk, or box. Bess usually had ropes tied around
60 her wrists. Houdini stood on top of the trunk while a curtain concealed,
or hid, his entire body. When the curtain was lowered, the assistant was

continued

standing on top of the trunk. Then the trunk was opened, and the audience saw Houdini inside the trunk.

How did he do this trick? The trunk had a hidden panel, and the
65 assistant could get out through that small secret door. Houdini then quickly changed places with his wife. Bess sometimes came out of the trunk wearing a different costume. Speed was very important in performing this trick.

Make an Object Disappear

Many magicians make objects disappear. David Copperfield made
70 the Statue of Liberty disappear for a television show. In this case, it is important to understand that this was an illusion for television. Copperfield set up two towers on a stage. These towers supported a huge curtain. The TV cameras and the audience only saw the statue between the towers. The curtain closed, and Copperfield told the audience that he had made the
75 statue disappear. When the curtain opened, the statue was gone.

Copperfield's assistants had turned off the lights around the statue and had turned on another set of lights. Helicopters flew around the second set of lights. The illusion was only possible because the cameras tricked the eye. The Statue of Liberty, of course, never moved from its location. The
80 cameras were simply positioned in a way that the statue was hidden behind one of the towers. Copperfield did a similar trick with a jet.

The illusionists Siegfried and Roy made an elephant disappear. The elephant, with Roy on its back, walked into a large box. Then the box was closed. When the box was reopened, the elephant was gone and only Roy
85 remained. In fact, the elephant walked out of the back of the box.

There have been many magic tricks and magicians in the history of show business. For some tricks, magicians make people, animals, and objects disappear or appear. For other tricks, magicians cut people in half or make objects and people **float** through the air. The tricks all have one
90 thing in common. The audience has to be willing to believe that the illusion is possible. In this way, we let ourselves be entertained and amazed.

MAIN IDEA

Every passage has a main idea. This is the most important topic or most general idea. Each paragraph also has a main idea. It is often in the first sentence, but not always.

D. Read the passage and answer the question. Circle your answer.

1. What is the main topic of the passage?
  A. how to make the Statue of Liberty disappear
  B. the first magician
  C. magic tricks and illusions
  D. the history of magic

✔ Look at page 129 for the explanation.

DETAIL

Every passage has many smaller, specific pieces of information that tell you more about the main idea. These are called **details**.

E. Read the passage and answer the questions. Circle your answers.

2. The cups and balls trick
   - **A.** uses three cups and three balls
   - **B.** may have come from ancient Egypt
   - **C.** is easy for beginners to do
   - **D.** all of the above

3. Which of the following is needed for the cups and balls trick?
   - **A.** fast hands
   - **B.** a television camera
   - **C.** a large trunk
   - **D.** all of the above

4. When the magician shuffles cards, what happens?
   - **A.** They are put in a trunk.
   - **B.** They are mixed.
   - **C.** They are cut in half.
   - **D.** They are put in a cup.

5. For the rope trick, the rope is in the magician's
   - **A.** coat
   - **B.** hat
   - **C.** hand
   - **D.** handcuffs

6. Which word below means the same as *change*?
   - **A.** publicity
   - **B.** location
   - **C.** audience
   - **D.** metamorphosis

7. Houdini was an expert at
   - **A.** training animals
   - **B.** making large objects disappear
   - **C.** card tricks
   - **D.** escaping

8. Many people consider Houdini
   - **A.** the best trapeze artist in the world
   - **B.** the world's first magician
   - **C.** the greatest escape artist ever
   - **D.** the world's most intelligent criminal

✔ Look at page 130 for the explanations.

INFERENCE

You can use details to make logical guesses. These logical guesses are called **inferences**. Often you have to think about information in different parts of the passage and then piece the information together.

F. Read the passage and answer the questions. Circle your answers.

9. Which of the following is **not** true?
   - **A.** Copperfield damaged the Statue of Liberty.
   - **B.** Copperfield's assistants helped trick the audience.
   - **C.** Television can trick people.
   - **D.** The lights were an important part of the illusion.

10. What can we say about Siegfried and Roy?
    - **A.** They used television cameras.
    - **B.** They put a jet into a large box.
    - **C.** Their elephant could escape from handcuffs.
    - **D.** They used a trained elephant.

✔ Look at page 131 for the explanations.

WORDS IN CONTEXT, PART 1

In every passage, you will often find words that are unfamiliar to you. Look for clues in the sentence or in nearby sentences to help you understand **words in context**.

G. Circle the answer that is closest in meaning to the words in boldface. Then underline the clues that helped you.

1. Houdini was able to **manipulate** the key with his hands and even with his teeth.
   - **A.** make
   - **B.** handle
   - **C.** find

2. For other tricks, magicians cut people in half or make objects and people **float** through the air.
   - **A.** move
   - **B.** learn
   - **C.** fit

3. Houdini became even more famous as a result of this trick and the **publicity** that *The London Mirror* gave him. The newspaper published many stories about the handcuff escape.
   - **A.** a special talent
   - **B.** the newspaper of a large city in England
   - **C.** information about someone in a news story

WORDS IN CONTEXT, PART 2

Sometimes the author gives a clue by defining **words in context**. The author might include a definition, an example, or a synonym. Sometimes the author defines a foreign word or a special term. Commas often set off definitions in context.

4. Underline the part of the sentence that defines *handcuffs*. Circle the comma.

   This trick uses handcuffs, the metal device that police use to hold a prisoner's hands.

5. Underline the example of a master illusionist.

   Master illusionists like David Copperfield can make the Statue of Liberty in New York City disappear.

6. Underline the synonyms in this sentence. Circle the commas.

   Houdini stood on top of the trunk while a curtain concealed, or hid, his entire body.

7. Underline the phrase that means the same as the term *hidden panel*.

   The trunk had a hidden panel, and the assistant could get out through that small secret door.

8. Underline the definition of *metamorphosis*.

   The word *metamorphosis* means "a change."

✔ Look at page 131 for the explanations.

SPORTS

BASEBALL

▲ An African American baseball team
in the 1930s

Answer these questions.

1. What sports are popular in your area?

2. What is your favorite sport?

3. What skills do you need to play that sport?

CHAPTER 1

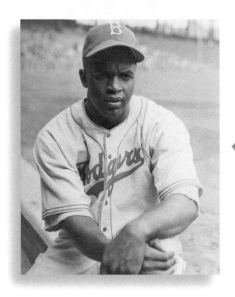

Jackie Robinson, 1919–1972

PREPARE TO READ

Discuss these questions.

1. Do you know the names of any baseball players?
2. What do you think makes someone a great baseball player?

WORD FOCUS

Match the words with their definitions.

A.
1. attitude ___   **a.** something that stops or limits someone
2. barrier ___   **b.** the effect on someone or something
3. impact ___   **c.** stop separating people and make them equal in an organization
4. inspire ___   **d.** way of thinking
5. integrate ___   **e.** make someone feel that he/she can do something

B.
1. prejudice ___   **a.** used to describe the separation of one group of people from the rest
2. radical ___   **b.** an unpleasant comment made to harm someone
3. retaliate ___   **c.** fight back
4. segregated ___   **d.** very different
5. slur ___   **e.** an opinion or judgment formed before learning

SCAN

Guess if this is true or false. Circle *a* or *b*.

Everyone was happy when Jackie Robinson joined the Brooklyn Dodgers.

a. True   **b.** False

Scan the passage quickly to check your answer.

Jackie Robinson: Breaking Barriers

Jackie Robinson changed the world of sports. Many people remember him as a great baseball player. More importantly, people remember Robinson as a pioneer. He was the first African American to play major league baseball.

5   Jackie Robinson broke the racial **barrier** in 1947. Before that, there were two baseball worlds: the world of the Negro Leagues and the world of the all-white major leagues. In 1947, Robinson joined the Brooklyn Dodgers. The Dodgers were an all-white baseball team from Brooklyn, New York.

10   When Jackie Robinson broke this racial barrier, it was a major victory. It gave Robinson the opportunity to have a wonderful baseball career. It also made it possible for other African American players to join major league baseball teams. Many people feel that Robinson changed sports forever. He also helped change American **attitudes** about race.

15   Jackie Robinson, who lived from 1919–1972, was always a great athlete. He was strong and fast. He loved to compete, and he was also intelligent. He watched every game closely. He always knew exactly when to make his next move. He went to the University of California in Los Angeles where he was a star in both football and track.

20   Robinson began his baseball career in 1945. He started playing with the Kansas City Monarchs. The Monarchs were a team in the Negro League. Word spread about what a great player Robinson was. Fortunately for Robinson, there was a new baseball commissioner named Happy Chandler. The commissioner is responsible for rules and decisions throughout the

25 league.

    In 1945, World War II ended. During World War II, African Americans fought next to white Americans. Commissioner Chandler believed that men who fought together in war could play baseball together. This was a **radical** idea. At that time, the United States was sharply divided along

30 racial lines. There were separate schools, restaurants, hotels, even drinking fountains. African Americans and whites sat in different places on buses and in movie theaters. The United States was a racially **segregated** country. Commissioner Chandler decided it was time for a change. It was time to **integrate** professional baseball.

35   The Brooklyn Dodgers selected Robinson to integrate baseball. On April 15, 1947, Robinson played his first game. He started at first base. People across the country talked about this event. They recognized it as an important moment in sports and in race relations in the United States. The major leagues had their first African American player.

40   Playing with the Dodgers was an enormous challenge for Robinson. Many fans didn't want him to play. They yelled malicious, or negative, comments, even when he made a great play. Players from his own team and from opposing teams felt Robinson should not be on the field. Players said racial **slurs**. They threw balls at his head, spat at him, and even

45 stepped on him. Robinson received several letters with death threats.

continued

What these fans and players didn't realize was how strong Robinson was. He was a strong player, but he also had a strong character. His coach Branch Rickey told him to ignore the negative words from fans and players. Rickey urged him not to **retaliate**. He advised Robinson to focus on the
50 game and ignore the people who wanted to stop him.

Robinson helped to make 1947 a very successful year for the Dodgers. Robinson was selfless and a great team player. He earned his teammate's respect. Robinson was named "Rookie of the Year." The Rookie of the Year award goes to the most outstanding first-year player in the league.
55 Robinson proved he could play great baseball even when other people were trying to get in his way.

Robinson continued to play well. He helped make the Dodgers one of the most competitive teams in baseball during that time. He was especially good at stealing bases. He watched the pitcher carefully and ran when the
60 pitcher wasn't paying attention. Stealing home is extremely difficult to do in major league baseball. Stealing home base scores a run, and the other team watches very carefully to avoid that. However, Robinson managed to steal home 19 times in his career. Most players can't do it even one time! He was named MVP, Most Valuable Player, in 1949.

65 During all his years with the Dodgers, life remained difficult for Robinson. Some fans and players still didn't want an African American player on the field. In addition, there were huge practical problems. When the team traveled, Robinson couldn't stay in the same hotel with his teammates or eat in the same restaurants. Segregation was the norm.
70 Robinson had to find another place to sleep, and he had to bring his own food. However, Robinson focused on the game and survived the barriers.

It paid off. His success with the Dodgers opened the way for other African American players to sign contracts with major league teams. He changed American sports, and he changed American thinking. He helped
75 shape the dreams of many young African Americans.

Robinson retired from baseball in 1956. After he left baseball, he worked in the Civil Rights Movement. He fought for the rights of all African Americans. During his years in baseball, he had faced **prejudice** every day. He had been denied his civil rights. Later, he became a voice for others. He
80 wanted African Americans to have the same rights and freedoms that white Americans had.

In 1967 Robinson was inducted into the National Baseball Hall of Fame. He was the first African American to receive this honor. He died in 1972 in Connecticut at the age of 53. Before he died, he wrote the
85 words that he wanted on his gravestone. These words reflect his experience in breaking the racial barrier. He wrote: "A life is not important except in the **impact** it has on other lives." He had a great impact on baseball and on the whole country. He became a symbol in the African American community. He **inspired** people, and he showed them how to overcome
90 prejudice.

Read the passage again and answer the questions. Circle your answers.

MAIN IDEA

1. What is the main topic of this passage?
   A. the Brooklyn Dodgers
   B. the Civil Rights Movement
   C. Jackie Robinson's career
   D. the history of baseball

DETAIL

2. What was most important about Robinson joining the Dodgers?
   A. He liked to play baseball.
   B. He also was a football star in college.
   C. He broke the racial barrier.
   D. He played in New York.

3. When did Robinson join the Dodgers?
   A. 1945
   B. 1947
   C. 1956
   D. 1972

4. When Robinson joined the Dodgers,
   A. his teammates were happy
   B. the fans were excited
   C. he made a lot of money
   D. he faced a lot of prejudice

5. Which did Robinson do first?
   A. win MVP for the Brooklyn Dodgers
   B. become Rookie of the Year
   C. work in the Civil Rights Movement
   D. play with the Kansas City Monarchs

6. How many times did Robinson steal home base in his career?
   A. 14
   B. 19
   C. 29
   D. 47

7. After he stopped playing baseball, Robinson
   A. became a football player
   B. taught college classes
   C. worked in the Civil Rights Movement
   D. owned hotels and restaurants

8. Robinson joined the Hall of Fame in
   A. 1947
   B. 1956
   C. 1967
   D. 1972

INFERENCE

9. What is true about Robinson?
   A. He gave up easily.
   B. He was selfish.
   C. He understood he was a pioneer.
   D. He didn't care about others.

10. The most important effect of Robinson's career was
    A. he always played great baseball
    B. he inspired other people to fight for their rights
    C. he stole home 19 times
    D. he played for the Dodgers for ten seasons

CHAPTER 2

Negro League players

PREPARE TO READ

Discuss these questions.

1. Why do you think the Negro Leagues were popular?

2. When Jackie Robinson broke the racial barrier, how do you think this affected the Negro Leagues?

WORD FOCUS

Match the words with their definitions.

A.
1. acceptable ___
2. bar ___
3. discrimination ___
4. enable ___
5. endure ___

a. make someone able to do something
b. the practice of treating a group of people with prejudice
c. deal with a painful situation for a long time
d. keep out; officially not allow something
e. socially or morally good enough

B.
1. form ___
2. insult ___
3. prevent ___
4. progress ___
5. unfortunate ___

a. stop something from happening
b. unsuitable; not all right
c. make something exist; start
d. develop and become better
e. a rude or an unpleasant comment

SCAN

Guess if this is true or false. Circle *a* or *b*.

The Negro Leagues began in the 1980s.

a. True   **b.** False

Scan the passage quickly to check your answer.

The Negro Leagues

The Negro Leagues operated in many American cities from the end of the 19th century to the middle of the 20th century. The leagues were **formed** because segregation **prevented** African Americans from playing with whites. African American players were **barred** from both major and 5 minor league baseball during that time.

Although the U.S. Civil War had ended slavery in 1865, segregation was a way of life in the United States. Well into the 20th century, it was part of every aspect of life, including sports. After the Civil War, baseball was invented, and it quickly became very popular. It was played all over the 10 country. Americans of all classes and races played baseball together. It was still an amateur sport at that time, so people didn't get paid to play.

All that changed in 1868. That year the National Association of Baseball Players voted to bar any baseball club that had African American players. No teams with African American players were allowed to compete against 15 teams in the National Association. Soon afterward, baseball became a professional sport. For a few years, African American players were still allowed to play on professional teams. This continued until 1883 when the Chicago White Stockings announced that African American players could no longer join professional teams. 1887 was the last year that they could 20 play. Talented players like Fleet Walker and his brother Welday Wilberforce Walker were forced out of professional baseball. Hundreds of talented African American players were denied the chance to play on professional baseball teams. This **discrimination** against African Americans eventually led to the formation of the Negro Leagues.

25 The Negro Leagues began in the mid-1880s. They lasted until the mid-1940s. Several smaller leagues played in the Negro Leagues. One was the Negro National League. It was formed in 1920 by Rube Foster. Foster is often called the father of African American baseball. The teams in each league played together all season. The champion team from each league 30 then played in a world series at the end of the season.

The Negro Leagues **enabled** African American players to play professional baseball. The leagues also provided entertainment for many African Americans. African Americans weren't allowed to attend major league baseball games. They couldn't go inside the gates of the major 35 league ballparks to watch the games. Segregation kept them out. Because baseball was such a popular sport, African Americans were eager to watch the Negro League baseball teams. All of the teams were very popular. Thousands of people went to the games. Families looked forward all week to go to a game on the weekend. Negro League baseball was big business 40 back then.

The teams in the Negro Leagues were very successful. Their success continued until the early 1930s. Money became a problem after the New York stock market crashed in 1929. Businesses everywhere were in trouble. This led to the Great Depression a few years later. Life was very difficult 45 during the Depression. Many people lost their jobs and could find no work. There was no extra money for entertainment like baseball games.

continued

Like everyone else at the time, the Negro Leagues had money problems. The leagues couldn't pay their players. As a result, the teams had to stop playing. The players put down their baseball bats and gloves and took other 50 kinds of jobs instead. The former players took any work they could find.

Then, in 1933, the economy started to improve. The players were able to return to baseball. First, a new Negro National League was formed. Then, in 1937, came the Negro American League. These two leagues played eleven World Series until 1948. They also played an All-Stars game 55 every year from 1933–1948. This was the biggest African American sports attraction in the country.

The Kansas City Monarchs were among the original teams in the Negro National League. This is the team Jackie Robinson played on when he started his baseball career. There were many other talented players in 60 the Negro National League. These included catcher Josh Gibson and the famous pitcher Satchel Paige. There was outfielder James Bell. He was known as Cool Papa. There were hundreds of skilled players. Many of these players have been forgotten over time. This is **unfortunate** because they were as good as the white players on the major league teams. Some 65 were much better.

The success of the new Negro League teams continued until 1947. In 1947, Jackie Robinson broke the racial barrier. He started to play for the Brooklyn Dodgers. He was the first African American player to join a white team. His move to the major leagues changed baseball for everyone.

70 Robinson's move affected the Negro Leagues. His success with the Dodgers paved the way for other African Americans to play for major league teams. Major league baseball started to become integrated. This was the beginning of the end for the Negro Leagues. African American players wanted to play on the major league teams. Over the next few years, many 75 of the best players in the Negro Leagues left.

Change came, but slowly. By 1950, only five of the 16 major league teams were integrated. By 1954, only seven percent of all major league players were African American. It wasn't until 1959 that all 16 major league teams had at least one African American player.

80 Many African American players, however, found that playing in the major leagues was lonely. It was lonely being the only African American player on the team. It was lonely sleeping in the team bus because hotels accepted only whites. It was lonely eating dinner away from the team, too. Players still **endured** racial **insults** from some fans. Other players 85 said unkind words as well. Even so, the best African American players continued to leave the Negro Leagues to play in the major leagues.

It wasn't until 1964, when civil rights legislation passed in the U.S. Congress, that African American players could finally sleep and eat with their teams. Integration in the United States was slowly **progressing**. By 90 the early 1950s, it had become **acceptable** for African American players to compete alongside their fellow man, and the Negro Leagues ended.

Read the passage again and answer the questions. Circle your answers.

MAIN IDEA
1. What is the main topic of this passage?
   A. the founder of the Negro National League
   B. why the Negro Leagues were formed
   C. important people in the Negro Leagues
   D. the impact of the Great Depression

DETAIL
2. In 1868
   A. there were no professional teams
   B. the National Association barred African American players
   C. the Chicago White Stockings barred African American players
   D. the Negro Leagues were started

3. Rube Foster was called the father of African American baseball because
   A. he had several sons who were baseball players
   B. he played baseball in the 1880s
   C. he organized a world series each season
   D. he started the Negro National League

4. Who were the Kansas City Monarchs?
   A. a rival of the Chicago White Stockings
   B. a major league baseball team
   C. one of the first teams in the Negro National League
   D. an All-Star team of great African American players

5. In 1937
   A. the Depression started
   B. the Negro National League was formed
   C. the Negro American League was formed
   D. players started leaving for the major league teams

6. Satchel Paige was
   A. a pitcher
   B. an outfielder
   C. a catcher
   D. a first baseman

7. By 1950,
   A. a few major league teams were integrated
   B. seven per cent of major league players were African American
   C. all teams had at least one African American player
   D. all the players could stay in the same hotel

8. What happened in 1964?
   A. Congress passed laws to end segregation.
   B. African American players could stay with their teams.
   C. Restaurants couldn't exclude African American players.
   D. all of the above

INFERENCE
9. In 1947, Jackie Robinson broke the racial barrier. What effect did this have?
   A. African American players wanted to go to the major league teams.
   B. The first world series was held.
   C. The Negro Leagues became stronger.
   D. all of the above

10. The biggest reason the Negro Leagues ended in the 1950s was
    A. the African American players were lonely
    B. African American players couldn't eat with their teams
    C. baseball was becoming integrated
    D. there were no hotels for African American players to sleep in

CHAPTER 3

◀ Pitching to the batter

PREPARE TO READ

Discuss these questions.

1. Why do you think physics is important in baseball?

2. What does a batter need to do to hit a home run?

WORD FOCUS

Match the words with their definitions.

A.

1. collide ___   **a.** decide something; influence what happens
2. covet ___   **b.** very important; what happens next depends on it
3. critical ___   **c.** best; most desirable
4. determine ___   **d.** strongly want something
5. optimal ___   **e.** crash violently into something or someone

B.

1. reduce ___   **a.** push with a sudden movement
2. soar ___   **b.** try very hard to get or do something
3. strive ___   **c.** move from one place to another
4. thrust ___   **d.** become smaller or less
5. transfer ___   **e.** fly very fast and very high in the air

SCAN

Guess if this is true or false. Circle *a* or *b*.

The hotter the temperature of the air, the farther the ball goes.

a. True   **b.** False

Scan the passage quickly to check your answer.

The Physics of Baseball

At first glance, baseball seems like a simple game. The pitcher throws the ball, and the batter tries to hit it. If the bat makes contact with the ball, fans eagerly wait to see what will happen next. They hope to see the ball **soar** out of the ballpark for a home run.

5   Many people have studied the mechanics of baseball because baseball is based on simple laws of physics. Let's start with the pitcher. The pitcher's main job is to deliver the ball to the batter. The ball requires *momentum* to get it there. Momentum is the force that keeps a moving object moving. The pitcher needs to move his body in such a way that he can **transfer**
10 momentum from his body to the ball. This is how it works. The ball starts moving when it leaves the pitcher's hand. The momentum from the pitcher's body must propel the ball forward. How much momentum the ball has will **determine** whether the ball reaches the batter at 80 miles per hour (128 kmph) or at 40 mph (64 kmph). To transfer momentum to
15 the ball, the pitcher first moves his body weight back and then **thrusts** it forward as he releases the ball.

   This movement of the pitcher is based on a principle in physics. It's called the *sequential summation of movement*. According to this principle, the largest body mass moves first, the next largest second, and so on, down
20 to the smallest. This means that first the pitcher moves his legs, then his hips, his arms, and finally his fingers. Each time he moves a body part, he transfers momentum from that body part to the next, for example, from his legs to his hips. If his timing and movements are just right, the ball will be fast and difficult to hit. The height of the pitcher also matters. If the pitcher
25 is tall, the ball has more *angular momentum*. A tall pitcher delivers the ball from a higher angle than a short pitcher. This makes the ball more difficult to hit. Both the speed and the angle of the ball influence what happens when the ball crosses home plate.

   Then there's the batter. If the bat makes contact with the ball, the
30 distance the ball travels is based on the angle at which the ball leaves the bat and how fast it is hit. How fast the ball leaves the bat is determined by the speed of the pitch and the speed the bat is swung. To understand the relationship between these speeds, imagine you are the batter and the pitcher throws the ball right at the bat, but you don't move the bat. When
35 the ball hits the bat, the ball bounces off with most of the ball's speed. Since you didn't swing the bat, the bat didn't help it move. The opposite is also true. If you hold the ball in one hand and hit the ball with the bat, the speed the ball moves is the result of the bat's speed. This is because the ball wasn't moving at all when you hit it.

40   When the batter swings, the bat and ball **collide**, and the speeds of the two come together within about 1/1000th of a second. The batter has to make a very quick decision about when to swing. The expression "it's all in the timing" definitely applies to baseball. If the batter swings 1/100th of a second too soon, the ball goes too far to the left. If the swing is 1/100th
45 of a second too late, the ball goes too far to the right. Reaction time is **critical**. The batter must hit the ball at the right time to get a home run.

continued

Why aren't all hits home runs? *Gravity* is one factor. Gravity is the force that makes objects fall to the ground. Gravity influences what happens to the ball after it is hit. If the batter hits the ball high up in the air, it stays
50 up for a bit and then it falls without traveling far because gravity pulls it downward. If the ball is hit low and straight, a line drive, it moves fast but not too far. It is close to the ground, so gravity pulls it downward and it stops. For a batter to get a home run, then, the ball must remain in the air for a long time, and it must travel a long way. It must move far over the
55 outfield and out of the ballpark.

Another factor is the air resistance, or *drag,* on the ball. Drag is the pull, or force, on an object moving through the air. The amount of air resistance on the ball is based in part on the temperature and the altitude. The higher the temperature, the farther the ball travels. For example, if a ball is hit
60 to centerfield, the distance it travels will increase by 4 feet (1.2 m) for every 10 degrees Fahrenheit (5.5 degrees C) of temperature. Likewise, the distance will increase by 7 feet (2.1 m) for every 1,000 feet (300 m) of altitude. As a result, a ball hit at the ballpark in Denver, Colorado, which is about 5,500 feet (1,650 m) above sea level, will travel about 35 feet
65 (10.5 m) farther than if it were hit in Boston or New York, which are both at sea level.

The particular spot on the bat where bat and ball collide is also significant. Batters **strive** to hit the ball on the "sweet spot." This is the **optimal** place to make contact because there is less vibration of the
70 bat. When the ball hits the sweet spot, the ball travels far in a seemingly effortless way. The shock of the impact of the ball is **reduced** so much that the batter barely feels it. The ball soars through the air.

Baseball seems like a simple contest between a pitcher who throws the ball and the batter who swings at it. But, basic laws of physics help
75 determine what happens once the ball leaves the pitcher's hand and makes contact with the bat. Under the right conditions, the ball and the bat come together at just the right angle, speed, and moment for the **coveted** home run.

Read the passage again and answer the questions. Circle your answers.

MAIN IDEA

1. What is the main topic of this passage?
   - **A.** why baseball is a simple game
   - **B.** how the pitcher throws the ball
   - **C.** the reaction time of the batter
   - **D.** the laws of physics in baseball

DETAIL

2. To get the ball across home plate, it needs
   - **A.** temperature
   - **B.** momentum
   - **C.** drag
   - **D.** gravity

3. What is sequential summation of movement?
   - **A.** the movement of the ball as it hits the bat
   - **B.** the movement of the player in centerfield as he runs
   - **C.** the movement of the batter at home plate
   - **D.** the movement from the largest mass to the smallest

4. Gravity makes
   - **A.** the ball go farther
   - **B.** the ball go faster
   - **C.** the ball drop
   - **D.** the ball soar

5. Which of these affect drag?
   - **A.** altitude and temperature
   - **B.** time of day and month of the year
   - **C.** height of the pitcher and the batter
   - **D.** the sweet spot and vibration

6. Which of the following determines how far a ball goes?
   - **A.** only the speed of the pitch
   - **B.** the height of the ball
   - **C.** only the speed of the bat
   - **D.** the speed of the pitch and the bat

7. How long does it take for the bat and ball to crash together?
   - **A.** about 1/10th of a second
   - **B.** about 1/100th of a second
   - **C.** about 1/1000th of a second
   - **D.** about 1/10,000th of a second

8. On a hot day, a ball will probably
   - **A.** go farther
   - **B.** not go very high
   - **C.** drop more quickly
   - **D.** stay close to the ground

INFERENCE

9. What is the main reason it is difficult to hit a home run?
   - **A.** The ball is going very fast.
   - **B.** The pitcher throws differently.
   - **C.** Everything must be right.
   - **D.** The weather is too cool.

10. When the batter hits the ball on the sweet spot,
    - **A.** the batter feels less vibration
    - **B.** the ball travels far
    - **C.** he has hit the optimal spot
    - **D.** all of the above

VOCABULARY REVIEW

WHICH MEANING?

From Chapter 1: *Jackie Robinson: Breaking Barriers*

1. What does *survive* mean in the following sentence?

> Robinson focused on the game and survived the barriers.

A. survive *(verb)* to continue to live
B. survive *(verb)* to overcome difficulties
C. survive *(verb)* to overcome health problems

From Chapter 2: *The Negro Leagues*

2. What does *operate* mean in the following sentence?

> The leagues operated from the end of the 19th century to the middle of the 20th century.

A. operate *(verb)* to cut open someone's body to fix something
B. operate *(verb)* to function as a business
C. operate *(verb)* to run equipment

From Chapter 3: *The Physics of Baseball*

3. What does *mechanics* mean in the following sentence?

> Many people have studied the mechanics of baseball because baseball is based on simple laws of physics.

A. mechanics *(noun)* the rules of writing
B. mechanics *(pl. noun)* people who repair machines
C. mechanics *(noun)* the way something works

WRONG WORD

One word in each group does not fit. Circle the word.

1. pioneer	barrier	first	start
2. threat	transfer	slur	insult
3. run away	escape	hide	endure
4. optimal	highest	acceptable	best
5. soar	fall	drop	gravity
6. segregate	separate	collide	divide

WORDS IN CONTEXT

Fill in the blanks with words from each box.

attitude	barred	inspires	prejudice	retaliate

1. Robinson didn't _____ when other players insulted him.
2. During segregation, African Americans were _____ from entering white ballparks.
3. The student didn't do well in school because he had a bad _____.
4. The teacher _____ her students to work hard.
5. There was a lot of _____ in the United States in the 1950s.

barriers	endure	formed	prevented	radical

6. Segregation _____ African Americans from playing in the white baseball leagues.
7. Jackie Robinson had to _____ many difficulties in his career.
8. Her ideas were _____ compared to those of the other students.
9. The Negro Leagues were _____ so that African American players could play.
10. The first people to do something often face _____.

collide	critical	optimal	reduce	strive

11. Some people think fall is the _____ season to travel. Others think spring is best.
12. The students always _____ to do a good job.
13. Knowing when to swing is _____ in baseball.
14. The two cars were about to _____, but one driver turned just in time.
15. Hitting the ball on the sweet spot will _____ vibration.

WORD FAMILIES

Fill in the blanks with words from each box.

acceptance *(noun)*	accept *(verb)*	acceptable *(adjective)*

1. It was difficult for African American players to gain _____ in the major leagues.
2. In the 1930s, it was not _____ for African Americans to play in the major leagues.

| discrimination *(noun)* | discriminate *(verb)* | discriminatory *(adjective)* |

3. After 1964, it was against the law to _____ against African Americans in restaurants.

4. _____ in baseball led to the formation of the Negro Leagues.

| endurance *(noun)* | endure *(verb)* | endurable *(adjective)* |

5. Professional athletes need a lot of _____.

6. Some people wondered how it was _____ for Jackie Robinson to be the only African American player on the Dodgers.

WRAP IT UP

DISCUSS THE THEME

Read these questions and discuss them with your partner.

1. What do you think makes someone a good team player? Can you think of a friend or famous athlete who is a good team player?

2. What types of discrimination and prejudice exist in sports right now?

3. If you know the physics of a sport, will that make you a better athlete? Why or why not?

4. What activities could you do to test out the laws of physics discussed in this unit?

RESPOND IN WRITING

Look back at the unit and choose the passage you enjoyed the most. Read it again. Write a one-paragraph summary of the passage in your notebook.

What do you think is the most interesting thing about this passage, and why? Write a paragraph in your notebook.

ASTRONOMY
SPACE EXPLORATION

An image taken by the Hubble Space Telescope

BEFORE YOU READ

Answer these questions.

1. Do you ever go out at night and look at the stars?
2. What do you think of space travel? Should we visit other planets?
3. Look at the photo. Describe what you see.

CHAPTER 1

◀ Edwin Hubble, 1889-1953

PREPARE TO READ

Discuss these questions.

1. What do you know about scientists like Copernicus, Galileo, and Einstein?

2. Have you ever looked at the stars with a telescope? What was it like?

WORD FOCUS

Match the words with their definitions.

A.

1. astronomy ___
2. contribution ___
3. destined ___
4. enlist ___
5. excel ___

a. sure to be, have, or do something
b. be very good at something
c. join the army, navy, or air force
d. the scientific study of the stars and planets
e. something that you give or do together with others

B.

1. galaxy ___
2. observatory ___
3. scholarship ___
4. telescope ___
5. universe ___

a. everything that exists, including the stars and planets
b. a large group of stars and planets in outer space
c. an instrument used to look at things from great distances
d. a building where scientists look at outer space with telescopes
e. money given to someone to help pay for studies

SCAN

Guess if this is true or false. Circle a or b.

Edwin Hubble was a Rhodes Scholar.

a. True   **b.** False

Scan the passage quickly to check your answer.

Edwin Hubble: A Man with a Vision

Edwin Hubble is responsible for some of the 20th century's greatest discoveries in **astronomy**. One of the most exciting inventions in astronomy, the Hubble Space **Telescope**, was named in his honor. His name belongs with great astronomers such as Galileo and Copernicus,
5 but few people outside the field of astronomy know about Hubble's **contributions** to our understanding of the **universe**.

Hubble was born in 1889. His early life was quite ordinary. There is little hint of the remarkable work he would eventually do. In fact, it appeared that Hubble was **destined** to be an athlete. Edwin Hubble was
10 like most young boys of his time. He delivered newspapers in the morning. As a boy, he liked to read. He especially enjoyed the adventure books of Jules Verne, which were very popular at the time. In high school, he **excelled** in math, science, and sports. His favorite sport was football, but he also ran track. He even broke the Illinois state record for the high jump.

15 When Hubble finished high school, he won a **scholarship** to the University of Chicago. He helped pay his expenses by tutoring, and he worked at several different summer jobs. His junior year, he earned another scholarship in physics. He also worked as a lab assistant at the university. As in high school, Hubble was a great student as well as an excellent
20 athlete. While he was in college, he played basketball and boxed. In fact, he was a champion boxer. People in the boxing field hoped that Hubble would become a professional boxer.

At the university, Hubble first heard of the work of the astronomer Dr. George Hale. Hale's work in astronomy inspired Hubble. Hubble
25 graduated from the University of Chicago in 1910. He earned degrees in both mathematics and astronomy. He then went to Oxford University in England as a Rhodes Scholar. At Oxford, he studied law, not his real love, astronomy, because of a promise he had made to his father.

In 1913, Hubble earned his degree in law. He returned to the United
30 States to start his own law office. He decided that law was boring, so after just one year, he returned to his true interest—astronomy.

In 1914, he began studying at the University of Chicago's Yerkes **Observatory** in Wisconsin. He earned a doctorate in astronomy in 1917. Then he received an invitation from George Hale to work at the Mt.
35 Wilson Observatory in California. This was a great honor, but, instead, Hubble **enlisted** in the army. Like many young men of the time, Hubble went off to fight in World War I.

As soon as Hubble returned from the war in 1919, he went to the Mt. Wilson Observatory. In fact, he showed up in his army uniform. At Mt.
40 Wilson he was able to use the largest telescope at the time. This powerful tool was the Hooker Telescope. It was 100 inches (254 cm) wide. With it, Hubble made some of the greatest discoveries in the field of astronomy.

Hubble made four major contributions to the field. First, he found that there were **galaxies** outside of ours. Second, he developed a way of
45 grouping galaxies. He could determine their age, shape, brightness, and distance. By grouping galaxies, he made his third finding. He determined

continued

that galaxies are separate and take up unique areas in space. Finally, his fourth finding was his most important. He found that the universe was constantly expanding, or moving outward. This last finding was a basis for
50 the "Big Bang Theory." The Big Bang Theory says that the universe started with one huge blast and is still expanding. That concept is somewhat like dropping a rock into a pond and watching the ripples of water moving out.

The great physicist Albert Einstein was very interested in Hubble's findings. Several years earlier, Einstein had presented his theory of
55 relativity. Hubble's work in astronomy seemed to support Einstein's theory.

When World War II started, Hubble again wanted to help his country. At first, he wanted to enlist in the army again. Eventually, he decided to serve his country as a scientist. He left the Mt. Wilson Observatory to work at the Aberdeen Proving Ground in Maryland. There, he helped to find
60 problems in weapons. Hubble was awarded the Medal of Merit by the U.S. government in 1946 for this work.

After the war was over, Hubble went back to his job at Mt. Wilson. He realized that the Hooker Telescope was strong, but not strong enough. Hubble helped design and build a 200-inch (508 cm) telescope. This
65 telescope, named after George Hale, was built at Mt. Palomar near San Diego, California. Hubble had the honor of being the first to use this exciting new telescope on June 3, 1948.

Hubble received many honors and awards for his efforts in the field of astronomy. However, he never received the Nobel Prize. He didn't
70 receive this award because there was no Nobel Prize given for the field of astronomy. Before he died, Hubble worked to make astronomy part of the field of physics. By doing this, he hoped to make it possible for astronomers to win a Nobel Prize. The prize committee finally decided to make astronomy part of physics. Unfortunately, Hubble, who died in 1953,
75 was no longer alive to see it.

In 1969, the National Aeronautics and Space Administration (NASA) started to think about building a telescope to send up in space. In 1977, money for the telescope was approved and building began. On April 24, 1990, the space shuttle *Discovery* was launched. On board, it carried the
80 first telescope that could float in space. There would be no interference from the Earth's atmosphere. This telescope, named the Hubble Space Telescope, has sent amazing images from space. Those images have helped us understand the universe.

Today, Edwin Hubble is remembered as one of the greatest astronomers
85 of all time. Hubble greatly expanded our knowledge of our own universe. His name belongs with other great thinkers such as Copernicus, Galileo, and Einstein.

Read the passage again and answer the questions. Circle your answers.

MAIN IDEA

1. What is the main topic of the passage?
   A. the development of the telescope
   B. the Big Bang Theory
   C. the life of Edwin Hubble
   D. the history of astronomy

INFERENCE

2. What was true about Hubble's childhood?
   A. His wealthy family traveled a lot.
   B. His father was a famous astronomer.
   C. He was sick most of the time.
   D. His life was fairly ordinary.

3. What did Hubble enjoy doing as a boy?
   A. writing for a local newspaper
   B. swimming and hiking
   C. reading books by Jules Verne
   D. collecting rocks

4. Hubble was a champion in what sport?
   A. football
   B. boxing
   C. basketball
   D. swimming

5. What did Hubble study at Oxford?
   A. law
   B. astronomy
   C. physics
   D. athletics

6. Which of the following statements is true?
   A. Hubble served in the army in both world wars.
   B. Hubble won the Nobel Prize in Physics.
   C. Hubble helped design the Hale Telescope.
   D. Hubble influenced Hale's work.

7. During World War II, what did Hubble do?
   A. He searched for problems in weapons.
   B. He was a captain in the army.
   C. He worked at the observatory.
   D. He was a spy for the government.

8. Which of Hubble's findings was a basis for the Big Bang Theory?
   A. It is possible to group galaxies.
   B. There are other galaxies outside of our own.
   C. Galaxies take up unique areas in space.
   D. The universe began with one blast and is expanding.

INFERENCE

9. What do we know about Edwin Hubble?
   A. He was a man of many interests and talents.
   B. He served his country.
   C. His work supported Albert Einstein's theories.
   D. all of the above

10. Which of the following statements is **not** true?
    A. Edwin Hubble invented the Hubble Space Telescope.
    B. The Earth's atmosphere affects telescopes on the ground.
    C. The Hubble Space Telescope gives astronomers better images of space.
    D. Images from the Hubble Space Telescope are sent back to Earth.

CHAPTER 2

◀ Mt. Wilson Observatory

PREPARE TO READ

Discuss these questions.

1. Have you ever visited an observatory?

2. What do you think are important considerations when choosing a site for an observatory?

WORD FOCUS

Match the words with their definitions.

A.
1. altitude ___
2. antenna ___
3. broadcast ___
4. clear ___
5. donate ___

a. send out a radio or television program
b. easy to see through
c. a tall metal structure used to send signals
d. give money to an organization
e. the height of something above sea level

B.
1. facility ___
2. ideal ___
3. magnetic ___
4. peak ___
5. transmission ___

a. the best possible; perfect
b. a building where a particular service is provided
c. the top of a mountain
d. having the ability to attract iron and steel
e. sending or passing something on

SCAN

Guess if this is true or false. Circle *a* or *b*.

A television station broadcasts from Mt. Wilson.

a. True   **b.** False

Scan the passage quickly to check your answer.

Mt. Wilson: A Mountain with a View

Mt. Wilson is a 5,715-foot (1,715 m) **peak** in the San Gabriel Mountains of southern California. It is located near Pasadena and Los Angeles. The **altitude** and the **clear**, dry mountain air made this a great location to study the night sky. With no city lights for miles around, the
5 dark night sky was perfect for viewing the stars and planets.

In 1889, Harvard astronomers chose Mt. Wilson as the **ideal** site for a new telescope. Mt. Wilson was on the opposite side of the United States from Harvard's Massachusetts campus. The Northeast had many large cities. In the 1880s California had few people. There were few city
10 lights to interfere with the dim lights of the distant stars. Because there weren't many lights, the night sky was darker. The sky was also clearer because there was no pollution from factories or smoky wood fires. Those things made California a better place for a new telescope than the heavily populated Northeast.

15 The Harvard telescope was removed 18 months later, but this wasn't the end of Mt. Wilson's impact on astronomy. In fact, it was just the beginning. In 1904, the Carnegie Institution of Washington gave $150,000 to astronomer George Hale to build an observatory on Mt. Wilson. Hale spent an additional $27,000 of his own money to build the observatory.
20 Hale had been working at the University of Chicago's Yerkes Observatory in Wisconsin. Hale brought the telescope from the Yerkes Observatory and installed it on Mt. Wilson. Hale also brought his team of scientists from Yerkes. Hale wanted to make Mt. Wilson the most important astronomical research **facility** in the world.

25 Mt. Wilson is home to a 60-inch (152 cm) and a 100-inch (254 cm) telescope. The smaller telescope was originally owned by George Hale. His father had given it to him as a gift in 1896. The larger telescope is the Hooker Telescope. It is named for John C. Hooker, the man who **donated** the funds to buy it. These two telescopes are used at night to observe our
30 universe. They allow astronomers to view stars and galaxies many light years away from Earth. A light year is the distance light travels in a year. A flash of light from a million light years away had to travel over a very great distance. It left its source millions of years ago. A flash of light visible in tonight's sky might just be reaching Earth from millions of light years away.

35 Astronomers have made many important findings at Mt. Wilson. One finding was that our sun is not the center of the Milky Way galaxy. Another discovery was that there are many, many galaxies. In the past, people believed that the Milky Way was the only galaxy in the universe. A third finding was that there is a **magnetic** field around the sun. This observation
40 helps explain why our planets revolve around the sun.

One of the most important findings made at Mt. Wilson is that galaxies are expanding. This finding by Edwin Hubble eventually led to the "Big Bang Theory." According to this theory, the universe began with a single enormous blast. After the blast, galaxies formed and kept growing outward.
45 Another major finding from Mt. Wilson was that some galaxies are older than others. This finding suggests that our universe is still growing.

continued

In addition to George Hale and Edwin Hubble, other major astronomers such as Harlow Shapley have worked at Mt. Wilson. Shapley found a way to measure the size of our own galaxy, the Milky Way.

50   Unfortunately, the growth of the city of Los Angeles has limited the usefulness of the Mt. Wilson Observatory. With so many lights in the surrounding area, the sky no longer gets dark enough for scientists to do deep space research. Also, the area has had major problems with pollution for many decades. Particles in the air make it increasingly difficult for the
55 astronomers to see things that are millions of light years away.

For the first half of the 20th century, the two telescopes at Mt. Wilson were the biggest and most powerful telescopes in the world. Then, in 1948, with the help of Edwin Hubble, the Hale Telescope was opened at the Mt. Palomar Observatory in San Diego, California. The Mt. Palomar
60 Observatory is 90 miles (144 km) southeast of the Mt. Wilson Observatory. It is owned by the California Institute of Technology. Mt. Palomar has four telescopes: the 200-inch (508 cm) Hale Telescope, a 48-inch (122 cm) telescope, an 18-inch (46 cm) telescope, and a 60-inch (152 cm) telescope. The Hale Telescope was the largest in its day.

65   While Mt. Wilson has seen more important discoveries in the field of astronomy, there have been some important findings at Mt. Palomar. In 1963, Maarten Schmidt used the Hale Telescope to search for objects too distant to be stars. He named these things "quasi-stellar objects." The shortened term for these objects is *quasars*.

70   Today, visitors to the Mt. Wilson Observatory can tour the grounds and can view the stars and planets through the telescopes. Visitors will also notice that many television **antennas** now stand on Mt. Wilson. After World War II, Mt. Wilson became an important location for television and radio **transmission**. In 1947, KTLA was the first television station
75 to **broadcast** from Mt. Wilson. Many television stations moved their transmitters to Mt. Wilson because the location makes it possible to use stronger transmitters and to reach more viewers.

Mt. Wilson is no longer the best place to observe the stars. Astronomers worry that the skies are no longer clear enough and the nights no longer
80 dark enough. No matter what the future of Mt. Wilson is, the scientists who worked there helped shape the way we think about Earth and our place in the universe.

Read the passage again and answer the questions. Circle your answers.

MAIN IDEA

1. What is the main topic of the passage?
   A. the history and development of the Mt. Wilson Observatory
   B. the different telescopes housed at Mt. Wilson
   C. the development of the field of astronomy
   D. the astronomical findings made at Mt. Wilson

DETAIL

2. Which university built the first telescope on Mt. Wilson?
   A. University of Chicago
   B. University of Massachusetts
   C. Harvard University
   D. California Institute of Technology

3. Who owns the observatory on Mt. Palomar?
   A. University of Chicago
   B. University of Massachusetts
   C. Harvard University
   D. California Institute of Technology

4. Why has the observatory at Mt. Wilson become less useful?
   A. The telescopes are too big.
   B. The telescopes are broken.
   C. There are too many lights in the area.
   D. all of the above

5. How big is the Hale Telescope on Mt. Palomar?
   A. 48 inches (122 cm)
   B. 100 inches (254 cm)
   C. 200 inches (508 cm)
   D. 60 feet (18 m)

6. What else can you see on Mt. Wilson?
   A. snow skiing
   B. transmitters
   C. power plants
   D. televisions

7. What other observatories are mentioned?
   A. Mt. Palomar and Harvard
   B. Yerkes and Harvard
   C. Mt. Palomar and Yerkes
   D. Yerkes and Wisconsin

8. What scientific discovery was **not** made at Mt. Wilson?
   A. the existence of many galaxies
   B. the existence of quasars
   C. the magnetic field around the sun
   D. the expansion of galaxies

INFERENCE

9. What do we know about telescopes like the Hooker and the Hale?
   A. They help astronomers see galaxies far away.
   B. They can detect light from thousands of light years away.
   C. They have helped change our understanding of the universe.
   D. all of the above

10. Which of the following statements is true?
    A. Our galaxy is the biggest in the universe.
    B. New galaxies may still be forming.
    C. All the galaxies are visible from Earth.
    D. All galaxies are the same age.

CHAPTER 3

The Hubble Space Telescope

PREPARE TO READ

Discuss these questions.

1. Describe the photo.
2. What advantage is there to looking at planets and stars from space?

WORD FOCUS

Match the words with their definitions.

A.
1. astronaut ___   **a.** a unit of computer memory equal to one billion bytes
2. atmosphere ___   **b.** not clear
3. blurry ___   **c.** expensive
4. costly ___   **d.** the mixture of gases that surrounds a planet
5. gigabyte ___   **e.** a person who travels into space

B.
1. instrument ___   **a.** a special task, purpose, or trip someone is sent to do
2. maintenance ___   **b.** the path a moon or another object takes around a planet
3. miscalculation ___   **c.** a tool that is used for a particular job
4. mission ___   **d.** keeping something in good condition
5. orbit ___   **e.** a mistake

SCAN

Guess if this is true or false. Circle *a* or *b*.

As soon as the Hubble Space Telescope was in orbit, it sent back perfect pictures.

a. True   **b.** False

Scan the passage quickly to check your answer.

A Telescope in Space

Astronomers are always searching for the best **instruments** and the best places to look at the stars. Over the years, astronomers have developed huge telescopes to improve their ability to view the universe. The larger the telescope, the better the view. One of the largest telescopes in the world is
5 200 inches (508 cm) across.

However, astronomers eventually found that after a certain size, larger telescopes didn't produce better images. The problem wasn't with the telescope. The problem was the Earth's **atmosphere**. Because the Earth is round, our view of the stars looks bent. Other things such as pollution
10 and light sources on the surface of the Earth also interfere with scientists' ability to see distant galaxies.

To fix this problem, astronomers suggested using a telescope in space beyond the Earth's atmosphere, moving around the Earth in **orbit**. Hermann Oberth first suggested this in 1923. However, this was at a time
15 when flight was still very new. No one had the ability to send anything into space. Lyman Spitzer presented the idea again in the 1940s. By that time flight capabilities had improved. It was no longer such a strange idea. Spitzer worked hard in the 1960s and 1970s to get the U.S. government to pay for a telescope in space.

20 In 1977, the U.S. Congress finally approved money for such a telescope. It was to be named in honor of the great astronomer Edwin Hubble. In 1981, the Space Telescope Science Institute (STSci) opened. It is a research center for the Hubble Space Telescope. Even after Congress gave the money, it took many years before the telescope was built. The Hubble
25 finally went into orbit 23 years after it got its funding.

On April 24, 1990, the space shuttle *Discovery* carried the Hubble Space Telescope into space for the very first time. The next day, the telescope was placed in orbit and began to operate. That same day, scientists noticed a problem with the mirror on the telescope. Pictures that came back to Earth
30 were **blurry**. This problem was very serious. Scientists didn't know if they could fix the problem. If they couldn't, the Hubble Space Telescope would be one of the largest and **costliest** mistakes ever made.

It turned out that someone had made some serious **miscalculations**— the huge mirror wasn't made correctly! Some engineers were working in
35 inches and some in centimeters. People had used the wrong measurements. The telescope couldn't be brought back to Earth to be fixed, so it had to be repaired in space.

It took three long years for the National Aeronautics and Space Administration (NASA) to figure out how to solve the problem. Scientists
40 decided the solution was to fit the telescope with mirrors, much like fitting a person with a pair of glasses. In December 1993, the shuttle *Endeavour* was sent into space to fix the telescope. Astronauts placed five new mirrors on the telescope, and the problem was solved. The telescope began sending back stunning images of distant galaxies.

45 The Hubble Space Telescope has several **missions**. Its first job is to explore the solar system. One task is to measure the age and size of the

continued

universe. It is trying to find clues to explain how the universe began and how it has changed. It looks at what happens between different objects in space under different conditions. Another goal is to answer questions about
50 specific stars, planets, and galaxies.

The Hubble is about the size of a school bus, and it weighs as much as a half dozen cars. It is in an orbit about 375 miles (600 km) above Earth. It takes 97 minutes to orbit the Earth. This means that it travels at speeds of about 17,500 miles per hour (28,000 kmh). If a car moved that fast, it
55 would take 10 minutes to travel all the way across the United States from coast to coast.

The Hubble runs on batteries that will last for about 15 years. NASA thinks that the batteries will last at least until 2009. Also, there are two 25-foot (7.5 m) solar panels that take sunlight and turn it into energy. This
60 energy gives some power to the telescope and its instruments.

It cost about $1.5 billion dollars to build and put the space telescope in orbit. It costs around $250 million a year to run. This includes data collection and analysis. It also includes the cost of continuing to develop hardware and software. The telescope requires regular **maintenance** to
65 keep its parts running properly.

The Hubble collects 120 **gigabytes** of data every week. It then sends the data back to Earth. Interestingly, the Hubble can't observe the sun or Mercury because that planet is too close to the sun. Also, it is impossible to get a clear picture of Earth from the telescope. The Hubble uses Earth to
70 take "test" pictures to make sure that everything is working properly. These pictures show no detail at all. The pictures are blurry because the telescope is moving so fast. It is like taking a picture from a moving car.

The telescope focuses on very far distances. So while it cannot see things close up, it can see things billions of light years away. In March
75 2004, scientists pointed the telescope in the same direction for several days. They were amazed to find at least 10,000 galaxies. Astronomers think that the furthest views seen by Hubble could be 12 billion to 13 billion light years away. A light year is the distance light can travel in one year.

NASA feels that the Hubble is too costly to maintain, and they may
80 simply abandon, stop servicing, it. The government feels that the risk of sending **astronauts** to service it is too great. Astronomers are extremely worried about the potential loss to our knowledge of the universe. They are fighting to make sure the Hubble continues into the future.

The Hubble Space Telescope has provided extraordinary images of the
85 universe. Edwin Hubble would be proud of what the telescope named for him has given to the world.

Read the passage again and answer the questions. Circle your answers.

MAIN IDEA

1. What is the main topic of the passage?
   A. why telescopes shouldn't takes pictures from Earth
   B. NASA's shuttle missions
   C. the Hubble Space Telescope and its missions
   D. how the Hubble Space Telescope gets its energy

DETAIL

2. When did someone first suggest putting a telescope in orbit?
   A. 1920s
   B. 1960s
   C. 1970s
   D. 1990s

3. The Hubble Space Telescope is as large as
   A. a football field
   B. an airplane
   C. a car
   D. a school bus

4. The Hubble telescope's primary mission is to study
   A. the Earth
   B. the sun
   C. the solar system
   D. Mercury

5. How long will the Hubble's batteries last?
   A. 10 years
   B. 15 years
   C. 20 years
   D. 25 years

6. What is a light year?
   A. the distance light travels in one year
   B. the time it takes for light to travel one billion miles
   C. the distance from the Earth to the sun
   D. the distance a star can travel in one year

7. When did the Hubble telescope start having problems?
   A. one day after it was put in orbit
   B. one week after it was put in orbit
   C. one month after it was put in orbit
   D. one year after it was put in orbit

8. NASA plans to abandon the Hubble because
   A. it is too expensive
   B. they don't have enough astronauts
   C. it does not produce good images
   D. it is too close to the sun

INFERENCE

9. Why was fixing the telescope similar to using a pair of glasses?
   A. The extra mirrors looked like glasses.
   B. The extra mirrors helped the telescope focus.
   C. The extra mirrors were thick.
   D. The extra mirrors were made of glass.

10. What will happen if NASA abandons the Hubble?
    A. Its batteries will continue working for 500 years.
    B. It will eventually stop sending images.
    C. The astronauts on the Hubble will have to come back to Earth.
    D. all of the above

VOCABULARY REVIEW

WHICH MEANING?

From Chapter 1: *Edwin Hubble: A Man with a Vision*

1. What does *finding* mean in the following sentence?

> By grouping galaxies, he made his third finding. He determined that galaxies are separate and take up unique areas in space.

A. finding *(noun)* the result of a court decision
B. finding *(verb)* locating something that is lost
C. finding *(noun)* the result of a study or an investigation

From Chapter 2: *Mt. Wilson: A Mountain with a View*

2. What does *stand* mean in the following sentence?

> Visitors will also notice that many television antennas now stand on Mt. Wilson.

A. stand *(noun)* a table or small store where things are sold
B. stand *(verb)* to be in a particular location
C. stand *(verb)* to be on your feet

From Chapter 3: *A Telescope in Space*

3. What does *fit* mean in the following sentence?

> To fix the problem, scientists decided to fit the telescope with mirrors, much like fitting a person with a pair of glasses.

A. fit *(noun)* a sudden period of activity
B. fit *(adjective)* in good physical health
C. fit *(verb)* to cause to be the proper size or shape

WRONG WORD

One word in each group does not fit. Circle the word.

1. astronomy	costly	mathematics	physics
2. gigabyte	galaxy	universe	space
3. antenna	transmission	broadcast	peak
4. telescope	view	enlist	mirror
5. miscalculation	magnetic	mistake	error
6. contribution	finding	discovery	observatory

WORDS IN CONTEXT

Fill in the blanks with words from each box.

astronauts	atmosphere	blurry	donated	facility

1. The images from space came back _____. They weren't clear.
2. The pollution in the air harms our _____.
3. Many children dream of being _____ and flying in space.
4. Several people _____ money to purchase a new telescope.
5. The research _____ was a large building with hundreds of scientists.

contributions	enlist	ideal	magnetic	universe

6. Hubble made several important _____ to the field of astronomy.
7. Many young men and women _____ in the army.
8. Mt. Wilson was the _____ spot for a telescope.
9. A compass works because of _____ pull in the Earth.
10. There are different theories about how the _____ began.

excelled	maintenance	mission	orbits	scholarship

11. The moon _____ the Earth once each day.
12. Hubble _____ in science as well as in sports.
13. Many people have made it a _____ to stop world hunger.
14. If I don't study, I'll lose my _____ because of bad grades.
15. Proper _____ will keep your car running smoothly.

WORD FAMILIES

Fill in the blanks with words from each box.

scholar *(noun)*	scholarship *(noun)*	scholarly *(adjective)*

1. His _____ book was both informative and well written.
2. He studies all the time. He's a real _____!

| excellence *(noun)* | excel *(verb)* | excellent *(adjective)* |

3. That university is known for its _____.

4. You did an _____ job on your exam. Congratulations!

| observatory *(noun)* | observer *(noun)* | observe *(verb)* |

5. Every day, we _____ the same car speeding down the street.

6. As an _____ he cannot participate; he can only watch.

WRAP IT UP

DISCUSS THE THEME

Read these questions and discuss them with a partner.

1. Would you like to travel into space? Would you be afraid or excited?

2. Do you think "space vacations" will happen in the future?

3. Should we spend money on space exploration or on helping poor people here on Earth?

4. Do you think there is life on other planets? In other galaxies?

RESPOND IN WRITING

Look back at the unit and choose the passage you enjoyed the most. Read it again. Write a one-paragraph summary of the passage in your notebook.

What do you think is the most interesting thing about this passage, and why? Write a paragraph in your notebook.

PHOTOGRAPHY
PHOTOJOURNALISM

Photojournalists at work

BEFORE YOU READ

Answer these questions.

1. Do you like to take photographs?
2. What do you take photographs of?
3. Have you ever thought about taking photographs for a living?

CHAPTER 1

Dorothea Lange,
1895-1965

"Migrant Mother"
by Dorothea Lange

PREPARE TO READ

Discuss these questions.

1. Describe the photographs.

2. What do you think the mother and children in the photo are doing?

WORD FOCUS

Match the words with their definitions.

A.

1. apprentice ___   **a.** succeed in representing something in pictures or words
2. capture ___   **b.** relating to a movie or photographs that give facts about a particular subject
3. documentary ___   **c.** a person who works for someone else to learn a job or skill
4. emotion ___   **d.** a collection of objects in a museum or art gallery
5. exhibit ___   **e.** a strong feeling such as love or fear

B.

1. migrant ___   **a.** show something in a particular way
2. portrait ___   **b.** a person who goes from place to place looking for work
3. portray ___   **c.** the place where a photograher or an artist works
4. studio ___   **d.** the person or thing that is photographed
5. subject ___   **e.** a photograph or painting of a person

SCAN

Guess if this is true or false. Circle *a* or *b*.

Dorothea Lange liked to photograph the rich and famous.

a. True   **b.** False

Scan the passage quickly to check your answer.

Dorothea Lange: Photographing Life

From an early age, Dorothea Lange could see the beauty and pain of daily life. Women of her day usually became teachers or nurses or secretaries. Lange, however, wanted to become a photographer. She never dreamed she would become one of the great photographers of the 20th
5 century.

Documentary photography was her main interest. In particular, she focused on social issues. She focused on the poor people in society. She recorded their problems with truth and care. She wanted her photographs to make the public aware of problems. She hoped to bring about positive
10 changes. But to do so, she had to be careful not to show just problems. She had to show all that made these people who they were. Lange was always sure to **capture** her **subjects'** pride, strength, and spirit.

Like so many great artists, Lange was no stranger to life's difficulties. Born in Hoboken, New Jersey, in 1895, Lange led a normal childhood
15 until age seven. Then she became ill with polio, a disease that was once very common. The disease affected Lange's legs, and she was left with a lifelong limp. At age 12, her father, a successful lawyer, left the family and never contacted them again.

After that, Lange's mother took a job as a librarian in New York City.
20 To be closer to their mother's new workplace, the family moved to their grandmother's house. Lange was very independent and loved to wander the streets of the city. The colorful scenes inspired her. As an artistic person, she felt the need somehow to capture what she saw.

By the time she graduated from high school, Lange knew she wanted
25 to be a photographer. She realized she had never taken a photo in her life. She also knew that women just didn't become photographers. But she held tightly to her dream anyway and decided to take a photography class. Shortly after, she walked by the shop of a **portrait** photographer, and he hired her to do work in his photo lab. Later, Lange served as an
30 **apprentice** to several other well-known New York City photographers.

Lange decided to leave New York City and move to San Francisco. It proved to be a wonderful change for Lange. In only a few weeks she met a group of friends. She also joined the San Francisco Camera Club. Because of the quality of her work, members of the club gave her money to open
35 her own **studio**. It became a huge success. She got to know many wealthy customers and friends, including a much older painter named Maynard Dixon. He became her first husband, and they had two sons together. Dixon helped shape his young wife's photography. He encouraged her to **portray** the difficult lives of his own favorite subjects: the men and women
40 of the West.

Soon Lange had a life-changing idea. She would focus her career on the hard lives of "real" people. In October of 1929, the stock market crashed, and this led to the Great Depression. Times were difficult for everyone in the 1930s. Lange could look out her window and see the poor people in
45 the streets. Because no one could afford to pay for portraits anymore, she had to close her business. So, much like in her New York days, she went

continued

out into the city to see the people. This time, however, she had a camera. She wanted to document the **emotions** in people's faces. She wanted to show how real people ate, how they gathered together, how they passed the
50 time. At a soup kitchen, where the homeless came for bread and hot soup, she photographed a broken man with a tin cup. This picture started a new path in her career and earned her much respect.

Like many working women, Lange felt torn between her family and her career. Her marriage wasn't working well. Lange and her husband decided
55 to send their sons to boarding school. She and Dixon moved to Taos, New Mexico, where they lived with a group of artists and focused on their careers.

In 1933, at an **exhibit** in Oakland, California, Lange showed her photographs. Her stark black and white photographs graphically
60 demonstrated the way the Depression had affected individuals. Her work struck home with Paul Taylor, an economist. He used Lange's photographs to make his reports on **migrant** workers more powerful. These reports actually caused the government to do something it had never done before: build housing for the homeless. In the meantime, Dorothea's success gave
65 her confidence to end her unhappy first marriage. She later married Taylor, and the two found much happiness together.

During this period in her life, Lange took her most famous photograph, "Migrant Mother." This photograph of a thin, tired-looking widow will forever be an icon, or symbol, of the Great Depression of the 1930s. With
70 this and other photographs, Lange became the most published government photographer of that time. Her photographs pushed the government to assist migrant workers and others affected by the Great Depression. Her photographs also inspired author John Steinbeck to write his famous novel about migrant workers, *The Grapes of Wrath.*

75 Lange continued to work for the government as a documentary photographer during World War II. By the 1960s, Lange was one of the best-known photographers in the United States. She had won many awards. She used her gifts as a photographer to help improve society. She also enjoyed a loving husband and closer ties to her two sons. But her
80 health was declining. In 1965, the Museum of Modern Art in New York asked her to agree to a "one-person" exhibit. She was only the sixth person ever honored that way, and the first woman. Lange accepted the invitation, but she died just three months before the exhibit opened. Nonetheless, the exhibit was very successful.

85 In her final words on earth, she called the timing of the exhibit "a miracle." If anyone knew about miracles, especially of the human spirit, it was Dorothea Lange.

Read the passage again and answer the questions. Circle your answers.

MAIN IDEA

1. What is the main topic of the passage?
   A. the history of photography
   B. life during the Great Depression
   C. a great photographer
   D. documentary photographers

DETAIL

2. What did photographs like "Migrant Mother" inspire the government to do?
   A. write a famous novel
   B. help migrant workers
   C. build schools for children
   D. hire more photographers

3. What did Lange enjoy doing in New York City?
   A. working in her garden
   B. walking around the city
   C. writing stories
   D. helping the sick

4. How did Lange afford to open her studio in San Francisco?
   A. She sold her best camera.
   B. Members of the Camera Club gave her money.
   C. She took photographs of very wealthy people.
   D. She saved money working as a schoolteacher.

5. Which of the following is true?
   A. Lange moved to Los Angeles when she was a child.
   B. Lange's first photo exhibit was in New York in 1965.
   C. Lange often photographed victims of the Great Depression.
   D. Lange met her husband at Columbia University.

6. How did polio affect Lange?
   A. The disease affected her eyes.
   B. She had trouble using a camera.
   C. It made her aware of life's difficulties.
   D. Her father wanted her to study medicine.

7. Which of the following is **not** true?
   A. Lange was married twice.
   B. Lange's use of color made her photographs famous.
   C. Lange had a serious illness as a child.
   D. Lange had the first one-woman show at the Museum of Modern Art.

8. When was the Great Depression?
   A. the 1920s
   B. the 1930s
   C. the 1950s
   D. the 1960s

INFERENCE

9. Lange preferred to take pictures of
   A. society's poorest people
   B. her husband and children
   C. farms and factories
   D. fashionable women

10. Why did Lange's photographs make Taylor's reports more powerful?
    A. Readers saw people they knew in the pictures.
    B. A picture is worth a thousand words.
    C. Lange was a better economist than Taylor.
    D. Taylor wasn't a good writer.

CHAPTER 2

◀ A farm in the Dust Bowl

PREPARE TO READ

Discuss these questions.

1. Describe what you see in the photo.

2. Do you know any farmers? What is their life like?

WORD FOCUS

Match the words with their definitions.

A.

1. choke ___   **a.** reduce the amount of something

2. deplete ___   **b.** a long period of time without rain

3. desperate ___   **c.** the time after sunset when there is almost no light

4. drought ___   **d.** not able to breathe; not able to grow

5. dusk ___   **e.** willing to do anything to change a terrible situation

B.

1. dust ___   **a.** a fine, dry powder

2. nutrient ___   **b.** a person who is harmed by something

3. prairie ___   **c.** be successful, especially financially

4. prosper ___   **d.** a large area of flat land with grass and few trees

5. victim ___   **e.** a substance needed to keep something alive

SCAN

Guess the answer. Circle *a* or *b*.

Route 66 connected what two cities?

a. New York and Los Angeles   **b.** Chicago and Los Angeles

Scan the passage quickly to check your answers.

The Dust Bowl

Imagine you're a farmer whose land has dried up. In fact, imagine that everything for hundreds of miles around has dried up. Soil that was once rich and dark has turned to **dust**. Overplanting has **depleted** the soil. For years, the entire region has suffered through a terrible **drought**. Crops
5 have shriveled. Cattle have died. You can't make enough money to support your family.

It's springtime now, and the usual winds begin to blow. The winds gather great force as they sweep across the flat landscape. The plains extend for hundreds of miles with barely a hill to break the flatness.
10 While you sit in your farmhouse and consider your hard luck, the faint whistling outside deepens into a roar. Suddenly, the world beyond your window grows dimmer. It feels like **dusk** instead of high noon. Huge dark, yellowish clouds swirl from the ground, higher, higher, till they're as tall as mountains. Thunder and lightning explode across the landscape. The air
15 seeping into your house smells bitter. You taste dust. Dust seeps around every window and under every door. Dust piles up inside the house in every corner, on every surface. It **chokes** every living thing.

When the wind finally dies down, you and your family go outside. The earth has become the air. The thick dusty dryness fills your lungs and
20 forces you back inside. There is little to do but wait for the air to clear. And it will—for a day or two, maybe a week, until another storm blows through. The next storm will surely destroy whatever hope you have left for your farm. Fear of the unknown keeps you there. You will stay on the farm until the winds blow away every bit of hope. Then you will pack up your family
25 and leave the only place you have ever known.

In the 1930s, photographers like Dorothea Lange documented scenes like this again and again. These terrible events happened in the Great Plains, a wide belt of **prairie** and farmland across the middle of the country. The Great Plains extend from Texas to North Dakota. This rich
30 agricultural region is often called the "breadbasket" of the United States. But in the 1930s, the region instead came to be known as the Dust Bowl. In one of the worst events in U.S. history, the soil turned to dust and literally blew away.

Droughts and winds had occurred before in the Midwest, but they had
35 never been so severe. During the 1920s, in fact, there was more rain than usual, and farmers **prospered**. But with this success, farmers became careless about the soil. They allowed their cattle to eat all the natural grasses down to the roots, and they overplanted the fields. They didn't let the land rest. The farmers made a lot of money this way, but they hurt the
40 land. The soil lost its ability to retain water and **nutrients**. When a seven-year drought began in 1931, followed by high winds in 1932, the soil began to blow away. The problem grew worse with each storm.

For instance, one three-day storm in 1934 pulled up over 350 million tons of soil in the West and Southwest. It dropped the dirt as far eastward
45 as New York City and Boston. Despite being 1,500 and 2,000 miles (2,400 and 3,200 km) away on the East Coast, these cities had to turn on their

continued

streetlights during the day so people could see through the dust. Another storm in 1935 destroyed the entire wheat crop in Nebraska, North Dakota, and South Dakota. That single storm swept away as much dirt as workers 50 had removed when they dug the Panama Canal.

The Dust Bowl forced over two and a half million people to migrate to other parts of the country. The hardest-hit areas were sections of Texas, Colorado, Kansas, and New Mexico. But the state that suffered the most was Oklahoma. Farmers in other Midwestern states also lost their farms. 55 Farmers could no longer pay their bank loans, and the banks took over the farms. The economic pressures created by the stock market crash of 1929 affected everyone. The Dust Bowl and the Great Depression left people **desperate** to support themselves and find somewhere to start their lives all over again.

60 Hundreds of thousands of **victims** of the Dust Bowl decided to move to California. Migrants from elsewhere around the country had also started moving westward to the Golden State. At the time there were no major interstate highways. Most people traveled along a now-famous road from Chicago to Los Angeles called Route 66. It is possible even today to follow 65 their path along parts of old Route 66. But it was a much harder trip back then. There were few gas stations, repair shops, and restaurants along the way. There were almost no motels to stay at either, but few people had enough cash for motels anyway. They slept outside and did what they could to cope with hunger and weather and truck problems. The trip could take 70 weeks or even months.

California wasn't what people had expected either. Rather than "the promised land" of their dreams, they found an overcrowded state. Many people were turned away at the borders. Those who were allowed into the state found that there were more workers than jobs. Most farmers were 75 able to hire workers for very low wages because so many newcomers were desperate and would work for almost nothing. The low wages made the newcomers' lives almost as hard as before they arrived. Even if an entire family picked cotton or fruit or nuts, they still couldn't support themselves. Some farm workers lived in houses with no floors. Children moving from 80 farm to farm weren't able to attend school regularly.

Slowly, in part because of writers and documentary photographers, the government worked to improve workers' conditions. People around the country reacted to the stories and images and pushed for change. Over time, conditions improved in the Great Plains as well. The drought ended, 85 and farmers learned from their mistakes. The Great Plains once again became the "breadbasket" of the United States.

Read the passage again and answer the questions. Circle your answers.

MAIN IDEA

1. What is the main topic of this passage?
   A. the causes of the drought in the Midwest
   B. the Dust Bowl and its effects
   C. agriculture in California
   D. life in the 1930s

DETAIL

2. Which of these was **not** a cause of the Dust Bowl?
   A. Cattle ate up the grasses.
   B. Farmers overplanted the fields.
   C. Farmers let the fields rest.
   D. A seven-year drought occurred.

3. Which of the following happened during the Dust Bowl?
   A. Farmers lost their farms because their crops failed.
   B. Farmers built larger farms and paid off their loans.
   C. Farmers in the Great Plains prospered.
   D. Farmers bought equipment to dust their crops.

4. Which of the following phrases best describes the Dust Bowl?
   A. winds blowing
   B. soil disappearing
   C. desperate farmers
   D. all of the above

5. How many people moved away because of the Dust Bowl?
   A. 100,000
   B. 2.5 million
   C. 66 million
   D. 350 million

6. What is the nickname of California?
   A. the Breadbasket
   B. the Land of Milk and Honey
   C. the Promised Land
   D. the Golden State

7. Which of the following describes a trip on Route 66 in the 1930s?
   A. There were very few motels, restaurants, or gas stations.
   B. Drivers could reach California in only a week or so.
   C. Hotels and motels lined the highway.
   D. The highway had four lanes in each direction.

8. In California, migrant workers from the Midwest found
   A. great opportunities
   B. better jobs and higher pay
   C. excellent housing
   D. none of the above

INFERENCE

9. Why is the information about Boston and New York included?
   A. to show that almost the whole U.S. was affected
   B. to indicate how far the dust traveled
   C. to help readers imagine how much soil blew away
   D. all of the above

10. Why did Dust Bowl farmers decide to move to California?
    A. They wanted to become movie stars.
    B. They wanted to see the ocean.
    C. California was a major farming state.
    D. all of the above

CHAPTER 3

Child laborers in a 1909 photo by Lewis Hine

PREPARE TO READ

Discuss these questions.

1. What do you think inspires people to become documentary photographers?
2. What is the main purpose of documentary photography?

WORD FOCUS

Match the words with their definitions.

A.
1. battle ___   **a.** something real that helps prove something else
2. breakthrough ___   **b.** an important discovery
3. evidence ___   **c.** a thing that is made for the first time
4. invention ___   **d.** a person who is the first to do something
5. pioneer ___   **e.** a fight between two armies in a war

B.
1. pose ___   **a.** cause an unpleasant feeling of surprise
2. prohibit ___   **b.** sit or stand in a position for a photo or painting
3. shock ___   **c.** an event that causes great sadness
4. tragedy ___   **d.** an event that causes great happiness
5. triumph ___   **e.** say that something is not allowed

SCAN

Guess if this is true or false. Circle *a* or *b*.

Photographers first began photographing battles during the American Civil War.

a. True   **b.** False

Scan the passage quickly to check your answer.

Documentary Photography

Documentary photography, or photojournalism, has helped create change in the world for over a century and a half. Now, more than ever, photographs tell truths about the world we live in. We can see these photographs in magazines and newspapers. We can view them in art
5 galleries and museums. With the Internet and digital photography, images can instantly touch the hearts of people around the world. In fact, the word *documentary* comes from the Latin *docere,* which means "to teach."

Photographs can move the heart and force people into action. Photographs document life by capturing a single moment in time. They
10 provide **evidence** and truth. They show viewers new people, events, and places. They show something honest about society, human nature, or life in general. They capture great **tragedies** and great **triumphs**. For historians, these photographs serve as records of times past.

Would you be interested in seeing a photograph of someone who lived
15 in the 1840s? It is possible. In 1839, two Frenchmen created the first photographic image. It was called a daguerreotype. This method made a direct image on a silver plate. It was an exciting **invention**. But there was no way to make copies of these early images. They were used only for portraits. Not until 1851 was it possible to produce photo prints.

20 Many people consider this **breakthrough** as important as the printing press. Photography soon changed how people viewed history and time. It even changed how they thought about privacy. The demand for photographs became great. Photographers started traveling around the globe hunting for exotic, or strange and unusual, images.

25 Just a few years later, photography made its way to war. Roger Fenton was hired by the British government in 1855 to shoot photographs of the Crimean War in Europe. British war reporters had begun to send back frightening stories of British troops dying from bad medical care and cold weather. Criticism of the government increased. To cover up the facts, the
30 government wanted Fenton to show the war in a positive way. Soldiers **posed** for Fenton to create scenes. Fenton produced over 350 pictures. He didn't photograph any dead bodies or any actual **battles**. Instead, he shot photographs of groups of officers who looked proud, brave, and happy.

Not until 1862 did most people see true images of war. In that
35 year, New York photographer Mathew Brady **shocked** Americans with photographs of dead Civil War soldiers. Brady was known for "getting the shot" on the battlefield. But he had a secret. He was nearly blind. Because he couldn't see well, he hired 20 photographers who did the actual work on the battlefield. His team's images were much more powerful than the
40 posed portraits of soldiers that people had always seen. Brady and his team captured the feeling of dozens of Civil War battlefields just after the battles had ended. Even today, Brady's images are a reminder of the war that nearly tore the United States apart.

Other early documentary photography was just as powerful. London
45 photographer John Thomson was a **pioneer** of the form. He showed the hard life of the poor working class in England in the 1870s. He took

continued

pictures of chimney sweeps, shopkeepers, flower sellers, and street cleaners. His photographs of these workers gained much attention. No one before Thomson had ever photographed social problems in England.

50 The goal of some documentary photographers was to convince leaders to change things. One example is Jacob Riis, an immigrant who spent his first three years in New York City without a job. He wrote articles and letters to city officials. He described the terrible living conditions of poor people in the city. City officials ignored him, so Riis took photographs
55 of the crowded living conditions, disease, and crime. Riis's 1890 book, *How the Other Half Lives,* caused historic changes. Future U.S. President Theodore Roosevelt, then the New York City police chief, saw Riis's photographs. Roosevelt started working for change. Politicians began to see the value of providing better housing and health care and of fighting crime.

60 Not long after, another American photographer, Lewis Hine, moved to New York City to help the poor. He started traveling the East Coast taking pictures of child laborers, or workers. He shot the children at work in factories and coal mines. He shot them at work on farms and fishing boats. His photographs from the early 1900s showed how very young workers
65 were treated. As a result of Hine's shocking images, the government passed laws to **prohibit** child labor. Additional laws were passed to improve public education for all children. Hine's photographs brought about social change and helped end child labor. This was the start of documentary photography in the 20th century.

70 By the 1930s, documentary photography helped reshape the policies of an entire nation. This was the time of the Great Depression. The American economy was extremely weak. Millions of people were jobless and suffering, in both cities and rural areas. Farmers had lost their farms. Other farm workers found themselves with no work. Helping people in
75 farming became the focus of the U.S. Farm Security Administration. This department decided to document the problem with photographs. This was the first time documentary photography was used this way.

A staff of well-known photographers such as Dorothea Lange traveled the nation and took pictures. The agency wanted the country's leaders
80 to see just how bad life had become for farmers and farm workers. The agency wanted the federal government to find ways to prevent this from ever happening again in the United States.

By the time the project was over in 1942, over 272,000 photographs had been stored in the government library for future research. Because of those
85 photographs, American life would never be the same. This was perhaps the greatest period for documentary photography in the United States. It resulted in a record of life at that time, one that still moves our hearts and minds today.

Read the passage again and answer the questions. Circle your answers.

MAIN IDEA

1. What is the main topic of the passage?
   A. the ways documentary photographers learned to take photographs
   B. how documentary photography influenced famous people
   C. how digital technology has changed photography
   D. the history, growth, and influence of documentary photography

DETAIL

2. The passage mentions which problem with daguerreotypes?
   A. They could not be copied.
   B. They were too small.
   C. They were only useful for people.
   D. The process was a secret.

3. In what year did it become possible to reproduce photographs?
   A. 1839
   B. 1851
   C. 1862
   D. 1890

4. Which people did John Thompson **not** photograph?
   A. bank managers
   B. chimney sweeps
   C. flower sellers
   D. street cleaners

5. After Lewis Hine took pictures of child laborers,
   A. more people hired children to work in factories
   B. thousands of schoolchildren wrote letters to thank Hine
   C. President Theodore Roosevelt made changes to improve housing
   D. laws were passed to forbid child labor and improve education

6. Mathew Brady was known for
   A. helping prevent the Civil War
   B. his posed photgraphs of proud, brave, happy officers
   C. taking the first true documentary photographs of war
   D. his ability to find good photographers during the Civil War

7. Which photographer influenced future president Theodore Roosevelt?
   A. Roger Fenton
   B. Jacob Riis
   C. Lewis Hine
   D. Dorothea Lange

8. The Farm Security Administration
   A. documented the lives of government workers
   B. hired Mathew Brady
   C. produced over a quarter of a million photographs
   D. all of the above

INFERENCE

9. Jacob Riis's efforts to help the urban poor
   A. never really brought about any positive results
   B. resulted from his jobless years in New York City
   C. caused him to earn millions of dollars as a photographer
   D. made him a popular speaker around the country about crime

10. Which of the following is true?
    A. Young children have never worked in the United States.
    B. Photographs can force change.
    C. Documentary photographers only shoot sad events.
    D. New York City has always been a wonderful place to live.

VOCABULARY REVIEW

WHICH MEANING?

From Chapter 1: *Dorothea Lange: Photographing Life*

1. What does *dream* mean in the following sentence?

   But she held tightly to her dream anyway and decided to take a photography class.

   A. dream *(noun)* a series of images during sleep
   B. dream *(noun)* something you want very much
   C. dream *(noun)* something that works very well

From Chapter 2: *The Dust Bowl*

2. What does *lost* mean in the following sentence?

   Farmers in other Midwestern states also lost their farms.

   A. lost *(verb)* to be unable to find
   B. lost *(verb)* to be unable to keep
   C. lost *(verb)* to get rid of weight

From Chapter 3: *Documentary Photography*

3. What does *move* mean in the following sentence?

   Photographs can move the heart and force people into action.

   A. move *(verb)* to cause strong emotions
   B. move *(verb)* to go to live in a new place
   C. move *(verb)* to make a play in a game

WRONG WORD

One word in each group does not fit. Circle the word.

1. portray	photograph	prohibit	pose
2. dusk	sunset	evening	drought
3. prairie	breakthrough	invention	technology
4. battle	migrant	war	soldier
5. portrait	emotion	studio	exhibit
6. tragedy	victim	desperate	triumph

WORDS IN CONTEXT

Fill in the blanks with words from each box.

breakthroughs	choke	dusk	shocked	victim

1. The _____ of the robbery called police to report the theft.
2. News of the terrible earthquake _____ the world.
3. She drove home at _____ and had to turn on the headlights to see.
4. Medical _____ in the past 100 years have saved millions of lives.
5. Watch the baby carefully, please. He might _____ on his food.

drought	dust	emotions	migrants	portrait

6. A large _____ of my grandfather hangs in our living room. It was done by a well-known painter.
7. The long _____ has finally ended. It rained all night long.
8. _____ from across the country moved to California looking for work.
9. He never cleans his apartment. There's _____ everywhere.
10. Anger and love are both very strong _____ .

captured	evidence	pioneers	studio	subjects

11. The photograph _____ all the emotions of the moment.
12. Children at play are her favorite _____ to photograph.
13. The painter had a large _____ with big windows and excellent light.
14. Police looked for _____ at the crime scene.
15. Dorothea Lange was one of the great _____ in documentary photography.

WORD FAMILIES

Fill in the blanks with words from each box.

prosperity *(noun)*	prosper *(verb)*	prosperous *(adjective)*

1. The Dust Bowl caused many farms to fail. Farmers who had once been _____ lost their farms.
2. Eventually, the drought ended, and _____ returned to the region.

document *(noun)*	document *(verb)*	documentary *(noun)*

3. Dorothea Lange wanted to _____ the lives of real people with her photographs.

4. We watched a _____ about migrant workers during the Great Depression.

desperation *(noun)*	desperate *(adjective)*	desperately *(adverb)*

5. She turned to her friends out of _____ . She urgently needed financial help.

6. The child was _____ ill and needed medical attention immediately.

WRAP IT UP

DISCUSS THE THEME

Read these questions and discuss them with your partner.

1. Describe some recent documentary photographs you have seen.

2. Where did you see these photographs? What did these photographs make you feel?

3. Imagine you are a documentary photographer.
   - What things would you photograph?
   - Where would you travel to?
   - What would your life be like?
   - What is the best way to show your photographs? In newspapers? Magazines? Exhibits?

RESPOND IN WRITING

Look back at the unit and choose the passage you enjoyed the most. Read it again. Write a one-paragraph summary of the passage in your notebook.

What do you think is the most interesting thing about this passage, and why? Write a paragraph in your notebook.

AMERICAN CULTURE
FOLK ART

The Mother Tiger Will Scramble to Protect Her Cubs by Thornton Dial, 1988

BEFORE YOU READ

Answer these questions.

1. How would you define "art"?

2. Do you have a favorite artist?

3. What do you think makes someone a great artist?

CHAPTER 1

Thornton Dial, 1928–

PREPARE TO READ

Discuss these questions.

1. Do you consider yourself an artistic person? In what ways?

2. Describe a painting or drawing you have done.

WORD FOCUS

Match the words with their definitions.

A.
1. collage ___   **a.** a picture made with materials such as paper and cloth
2. confident ___   **b.** relating to a traditional style
3. contemporary ___   **c.** put something in a place where people will see it
4. display ___   **d.** feeling sure about your abilities
5. folk ___   **e.** modern

B.
1. formal ___   **a.** a work of art made from stone, wood, clay, or other materials
2. mainstream ___   **b.** having a lot of experience of the world
3. sculpture ___   **c.** according to the usual standard or definition
4. sophisticated ___   **d.** an object that represents an idea
5. symbol ___   **e.** the way that most people think or behave

SCAN

Guess if this is true or false. Circle *a* or *b*.

Dial and his sons made wood furniture.

a. True   **b.** False

Scan the passage quickly to check your answer.

Thornton Dial: Folk Artist

For most of his life, Thornton Dial knew nothing of the definition of "art." He had always enjoyed creating what he called "things" with his hands. He hadn't thought to give his work a more **sophisticated** label. Certainly, he never thought to call himself an artist. And yet, he is today
5 considered a powerfully creative **folk** artist. His work is **displayed** in homes, public buildings, and museums around the country.

Dial's lack of **formal** training places him within a special group of American artists. These artists are called "self-taught" or "outsider" artists. They are very different from "art school" artists. Art school, or
10 **mainstream**, artists have usually lived in big cultural centers like New York, Chicago, and Atlanta. Mainstream artists spend years studying the masters, history's great artists. Most mainstream artists spend countless hours in museums studying great masterpieces and learning the masters' styles. The "self-taught" artists like Dial, however, have usually lived in
15 rural places. These artists develop styles mostly on their own, influenced by other artists like themselves. They are "outside" the usual influences in the art world. Not surprisingly, many folk artists have come from the American South. This is a region that has struggled with poverty, race, and other issues. It has given both artists and writers much to focus on.

20 Born in 1928 in Emelle, Alabama, Dial's early life was hard. His mother raised him by herself. Dial received little education and started working at a very young age. As a teenager, his mother sent him to live with a great-aunt in Bessemer, Alabama, an industrial town. There, he continued laboring at various odd jobs. These jobs all involved working
25 with his hands. At one time or another, he worked as a welder, bricklayer, carpenter, concrete worker, and housepainter.

After a time, Dial went to work at the Pullman Standard Company. Pullman made railroad cars. For most of the next 30 years he worked in Pullman's Alabama factory. During this time, he also raised a family.
30 Eventually, with his two grown sons, who also had been working at Pullman, he started a small business. He was 55 years old by then and semi-retired. Thornton Dial and his sons made lawn furniture. They made chairs and tables from steel and painted them.

For the first time, he also committed himself more seriously to
35 producing his imaginative "things." He wanted nothing more than the pleasure of creating. In these personal projects, he started to experiment with a wide variety of materials. These included metal, wood, canvas, and sometimes, plastics. He even used random objects he found next to the road or in junk heaps. When he needed more materials to work with, he
40 often just recycled, or used, his old projects. When his yard became too full of things, he buried the extra materials.

Though it is difficult to believe, Dial often buried his completed artworks, too. He did this because he felt embarrassed. His family and friends often laughed at his unique creations. Like Dial, they had never
45 thought about the word "art." The **sculptures** he made with everyday

continued

scraps and junk seemed strange to them, something their old Dial did to pass the time.

But secretly, Dial continued to build his projects until he became more and more **confident**. By the mid-1980s, he had found the confidence to
50 start displaying some of his works in his yard. These were basically true-to-form constructions. They looked like the real object but were made of unusual materials. For example, he made two deer from wood, tin, wire, paint, and other materials he had found. Dial's "things" were similar in spirit to the work of many other self-taught artists.

55 But it was soon clear that Dial wasn't quite the same as other self-taught artists. He had the ability to grow very quickly as an artist and thinker. He refused to remain stuck working in one kind of style or subject matter. He soon began experimenting with a variety of methods and topics. In 1987, he started working a lot with paint. He produced giant **collages** that told
60 stories with personal, political, historical, and social themes. His themes reflect his life as an African American in the South. His visual stories often had both human and animal figures, especially tigers. Tigers became his favorite **symbol** of the African American.

Still, Dial's work remained unknown until the late 1980s. In that year an
65 art collector named Bill Arnett made the two-hour drive from his home in Atlanta, Georgia to Bessemer. A friend had advised Arnett to look at Dial's work. Dial's talent amazed Arnett. He soon began buying Dial's "things." Not long after, he began to introduce Dial to other artists and to the folk art world.

70 Within a few years, members of the mainstream art world in places like Atlanta and New York began to see Dial as a man of great talent. They recognized the rich symbolism and historical content of his paintings and sculptures. People came to appreciate his art on many different levels. For example, in 1993, Dial's work was shown at *both* the Museum of
75 **Contemporary** Folk Art and The New Museum for Contemporary Art. It was a very unusual achievement. Folk art is rarely shown in mainstream art museums.

Dial's success and Bill Arnett's faith in him have been good for both men. Some of Dial's paintings now sell for well over one hundred thousand
80 dollars. Major cities have hired Dial to make sculptures and paintings. Important museums like the Whitney in New York, the Smithsonian in Washington, D.C., and the High in Atlanta have added his works to their collections. The professional basketball team in Atlanta hired Dial to paint a large mural for their arena.

85 When Thornton Dial began making his "things" so many years ago, he never dreamed that he would one day have the respect of the art world. He also never dreamed that people would pay him for his art. Perhaps even more telling, Dial's family back in Alabama now all spend time creating art. No one is laughing anymore.

Read the passage again and answer the questions. Circle your answers.

MAIN IDEA

1. What is the main topic of this passage?
   A. the challenges in creating folk art
   B. African American life in the South
   C. a folk artist's path to success
   D. American folk art museums

DETAIL

2. When Dial's yard became too full, he would
   A. advertise and sell his extra materials
   B. sell the artwork taking up space in the yard
   C. gather and burn all the wood
   D. bury the extra materials

3. Which of the following jobs did Dial **not** have?
   A. welder
   B. plumber
   C. carpenter
   D. housepainter

4. Which of the following describes Dial as an artist?
   A. self-taught
   B. outsider
   C. folk
   D. all of the above

5. Which of the following is true?
   A. Folk artists often major in art in college.
   B. Dial paid Bill Arnett to show his work.
   C. Bears were the important symbols in Dial's work.
   D. Dial created a painting for a basketball arena.

6. Thornton Dial started a small business with the help of
   A. the Pullman Standard Company
   B. his grown sons
   C. Bill Arnett
   D. investors in New York

7. Which of the following did Dial **not** make?
   A. collages
   B. sculptures
   C. photographs
   D. murals

8. What can we say about Dial's work?
   A. It has been of little interest to the art world.
   B. It has not yet been shown in major museums.
   C. It is rich in historical content and symbolism.
   D. It has no special meaning.

INFERENCE

9. Dial's family eventually realized that
   A. his "things" were quite valuable
   B. he wanted them to do his work for him
   C. he was a great basketball player
   D. all of the above

10. Bill Arnett introduced Dial to other artists
    A. because he believed it would help Dial grow as an artist
    B. so Dial could have people to socialize with in the big cities
    C. because Dial could teach them how to paint
    D. so Dial could team up with them to create great works of art

CHAPTER 2

Atlanta, Georgia ▶

◀ A house in Charleston, South Carolina

PREPARE TO READ

Discuss these questions.

1. Can you name some of the states in the South of the U.S.?
2. What do you know about the city of Atlanta, Georgia?

WORD FOCUS

Match the words with their definitions.

A.
1. construction ___
2. debate ___
3. extend ___
4. headquarters ___
5. hospitality ___

a. talk expressing different opinions
b. the central office of a business
c. being friendly and helpful to guests
d. continue from one point to another
e. building things such as homes or offices

B.
1. humid ___
2. isolated ___
3. phenomenal ___
4. split ___
5. unspoiled ___

a. having a lot of water; damp
b. unusual because it is so good or large
c. break into two parts
d. not damaged
e. not connected with others

SCAN

Guess if this is true or false. Circle a or b.

Memphis is the biggest city in the South.

a. True   **b.** False

Scan the passage quickly to check your answer.

The American South

The South has always been a fascinating region of the United States. The South's history, culture, and climate are very different from the North's. The North fought to end slavery. The South fought to continue slavery. The North had many large population centers and ports. The
5 South was mainly rural and relatively **isolated**. Northern winters were snowy and cold. Southern winters were mild, but summers were hot and **humid**. In some ways, it is no wonder that the North and the South once almost **split** into two different countries.

The past few decades have brought important changes to the South,
10 several starting in the 1960s. The most important change was the Civil Rights Movement. It helped bring about great social change in the South. African Americans had endured years of racism after slavery ended. Slowly, laws changed. Eventually, attitudes began to change as well.

Also in the 1960s, the U.S. government was expanding the system of
15 interstate highways. The interstates helped connect the South with other parts of the country. The growing system of highways connected smaller towns with each other. At about the same time, people began to install air conditioning in more buildings. People from other parts of the country began to see the South as a desirable place to live. People began to talk
20 about "the New South."

There has always been some **debate** about which states make up "the South." Does it **extend** as far north as Maryland? Does it go as far west as Louisiana and Texas? Most agree that the South, or the Deep South, as it is also known, includes the six states in the southeast corner of the country:
25 Mississippi, Alabama, Tennessee, North Carolina, South Carolina, and Georgia.

One factor in the development of the New South has been the **phenomenal** growth of Atlanta, Georgia. Atlanta is the region's largest city. It has the world's busiest airport, which helps fuel business activity
30 around the region. It serves as the **headquarters** for well-known global companies like Coca-Cola, CNN, Home Depot, and Holiday Inn. The city hosted the 1996 Summer Olympics. Professional teams in all the major U.S. sports—baseball, football, and basketball—call Atlanta home. Newcomers and visitors love the city's mild winters, friendly people, and
35 rich, diverse culture.

Like Atlanta, the rest of the South attracts newcomers from all over the United States and the world. The South has been the fastest-growing region of the United States for years. Housing prices are lower than in places like New York and California. Lower costs make the South attractive
40 to businesses.

New **construction** has changed the landscape of the South, but much of the natural scenery remains beautifully **unspoiled**. Visitors find lush green forests or white sandy beaches with warm clear blue-green water. Lovely old Southern homes are reminders of the 19th century, when cotton was king.

45 Visitors frequently comment on the famous "Southern **hospitality**." Even in large cities, strangers smile and say hello as they pass on the street.

continued

There are exceptions, of course, but waiters and clerks tend to be friendly. A routine trip to the store might include a long, friendly conversation about the summer heat, sports, or politics.

50 Southerners enjoy their own unique cuisine, or foods. Grits, which is ground cornmeal mixed with hot milk and butter, has been popular since the 18th century. Georgia is famous for its peaches and is called "the Peach State." Fried chicken, barbecued pork and beef, seafood gumbo, fried catfish, cornbread, black-eyed peas, boiled peanuts, and pecan pie are
55 famous dishes. Many Southern foods such as peanuts and okra, a type of vegetable, are of African origin.

In the days before air conditioning and television, Southerners often spent evenings on the front porch, drinking iced tea and telling stories. A large front porch with a rocking chair is an enduring image of the South.
60 People rocked and told stories. The South has produced great storytellers. Famous Southern authors include William Faulkner (1897–1962), Flannery O'Connor (1925–1964), and Thomas Wolfe (1900–1938). Although he was born in Missouri, Mark Twain (1835–1910) was perhaps the greatest of all American storytellers. Twain wrote about life along the
65 Mississippi River.

The South has also produced great storytellers in the form of musicians, artists, and politicians. Much of American folk art has its roots in the South. Artists like Thornton Dial tell the stories of life in the South in their paintings, collages, and sculptures.

70 The South has always played a major role in national politics. Candidates traditionally don't win the election for president without winning the Southern states. The Southern states tend to vote as a unified block.

Of course, the most famous example of Southern unity was the Civil War. In the 1850s, industry was growing in the North. Northerners were
75 actively working to end slavery in the South. Wealthy Southern landowners wanted to continue the way of life they had always known. This included owning slaves. Slaves did most of the work—and they did it without getting paid. Life was good for wealthy Southerners. They weren't interested in changing anything. In 1860, the South decided to separate from the rest of
80 the country and call themselves the Confederate States of America.

Millions of poor white Southerners had little to gain economically from the separation. They were proud of their differences with the North. They felt deep pride about their region, and they wanted to fight against the North. In 1861, the nation found itself at war North against South.

85 The Civil War ended in 1865. This terrible war nearly tore apart the country. Fortunately, for the good of humanity and the nation, President Abraham Lincoln and his Union Army were able to defeat the Confederates. Slavery ended and the country was reunited.

Southern pride lives on in the New South. Southerners still see
90 themselves very differently from Northerners. Northerners have turned to the South for economic opportunities and a warmer climate in winter, and the South has welcomed the newcomers with its hospitality.

Read the passage again and answer the questions. Circle your answers.

MAIN IDEA

1. What is the main topic of this passage?
   A. the ways the South has influenced the world
   B. the Civil Rights Movement in the South
   C. business development in the South
   D. the character, history, and growth of the South

DETAIL

2. Atlanta has the world's
   A. biggest factory
   B. first art museum
   C. busiest airport
   D. all of the above

3. What does grits consist of?
   A. ground pecans, peanuts, and sugar
   B. chicken, salt, and butter
   C. ground cornmeal, hot milk, and butter
   D. catfish, barbecued pork, and salt

4. Which of the following was **not** a famous Southern author?
   A. Ernest Hemingway
   B. William Faulker
   C. Thomas Wolfe
   D. Flannery O'Connor

5. Which of the following is associated with storytelling?
   A. fried chicken
   B. professional football
   C. interstate highways
   D. rocking chairs

6. What happened in the North before the Civil War?
   A. People worked to end slavery.
   B. Farms became more common than factories.
   C. The North wanted to separate from the South.
   D. The Northern states formed the Confederate States of America.

7. How did the South react to what was happening in the North in the 1850s?
   A. The South decided to end slavery.
   B. The Southern states built more factories than the Northern states.
   C. The Southern states wanted to form their own country.
   D. Southerners fought for Abraham Lincoln's Union army.

8. Which of the following is an example of Southern hospitality?
   A. making friendly conversation
   B. saying hello on the street
   C. a nice restaurant server
   D. all of the above

INFERENCE

9. People have recently been moving to Atlanta because
   A. they like the Atlanta sports teams
   B. they enjoy eating barbecue and pecan pie
   C. they drink a lot of Coca-Cola
   D. jobs and good housing are available

10. Why did air conditioning improve life in the South so much?
    A. It made the work environment more comfortable.
    B. It meant people could heat their homes in the winter.
    C. It meant people didn't have to talk about the weather anymore.
    D. It made it easier to stop and talk to people on the street.

CHAPTER 3

◀ A giant bottle-shaped piece of art in Finster's garden

Discuss these questions.

1. Describe what you see in the photograph.

2. Do you know any artists? Describe that artist's personality.

WORD FOCUS

Match the words with their definitions.

A.

1. art dealer ___
2. bright ___
3. collector ___
4. concept ___
5. craft ___

a. an idea
b. a person who buys many similar things
c. an activity that requires skill with the hands
d. a person who buys and sells art as a business
e. used to describe strong color

B.

1. evolve ___
2. generation ___
3. originate ___
4. pattern ___
5. technique ___

a. a group of people living during the same time
b. an arrangement of lines, shapes, or colors
c. develop
d. a particular way of doing something
e. start

SCAN

Guess if this is true or false. Circle *a* or *b*.

A German term for folk art is *l'art brut.*

a. True   **b.** False

Scan the passage quickly to check your answer.

American Folk Art

What makes something "art"? Is it the artist's purpose for the work? Is it the feelings or thoughts we have when we look at a creation? Is the artist's training important? Or can anyone, anywhere make art? One thing is certain: art is a way for people to express themselves through actions,
5 words, sounds, images, colors, or materials.

Many folk artists paint, but the paintings don't look like the ones that we usually see in museums. Folk artists are self-taught. They express their feelings in whatever way seems natural. They aren't concerned about and don't know "rules" about form. Relative size isn't important. A folk artist
10 might paint a farm where a chicken is nearly as big as a horse and a man is almost as big as a barn. There isn't much mixing of colors to produce light and dark shades. Colors are often **bright**, just as they come from the tube of paint. Reds, blues, greens, and yellows make many of these paintings lively.

15 The images in the paintings tell a story. The theme of the art is what is important. Folk art is down-to-earth. It reflects simple wisdom and old-fashioned values. Often, folk artists use their work to celebrate important events in people's lives. Births, birthdays, weddings, and funerals have all been favorite subjects of folk artists. Folk artists also portray the
20 everyday activities in their lives. We see paintings of women hanging clothes on a line to dry or men chopping wood.

For other folk artists, the materials make their work unique. A creation might use natural objects such as shells, interesting stones, and feathers. A collage or sculpture might use scraps of metal, wood, carpet, rope,
25 brick, and paper. Leftover, or unwanted, pieces of material are all around us. Many folk artists recycled even before the **concept** of recycling had a name. A creation might include common, everyday objects like bottles, cans, shoes, street signs, buttons, shopping carts, milk cartons, and many, many other things. What makes a person an artist is an eye for turning
30 common objects into works with meaning.

American folk art **evolved** from 18th- and 19th-century **crafts**. The crafts included woodcarving, ceramics, basketweaving, and metalworking. Wooden objects were often painted or carved to make them more attractive. Ceramic bowls and water jugs were made in interesting shapes
35 and with beautiful colors. Baskets were made in unusual shapes, with different materials and **patterns**. Metal objects made for use in the home had unique forms and patterns as well.

Many of these early craft forms **originated** in Africa. When African slaves first arrived in North America during the early 1600s, they made
40 everyday objects the same way they had in Africa. Over the **generations**, many of these earlier African influences remained. At the same time, new elements were added and new styles evolved.

It isn't surprising that African slaves were producers of folk art. By definition, folk art comes from a people, or folk, who are cut off from the
45 rest of society in certain ways. The artists might be isolated because of

continued

income, race, or culture, or simply by the place they live. All folk artists share two things in common: they have no formal training in art and they work naturally, in their own way.

For years, people have discussed whether folk art is really art at all.
50 Many people have called it a craft. Other people think that folk art is actually the purest form of art because folk artists express what they think or feel in their own way. They don't worry about what **techniques** they use or how they use them.

People even disagree about what to call folk art. Some who admire this
55 kind of art claim the word "folk" is insulting. In recent years, new names have been suggested such as "outsider art" or "self-taught art." Foreign terms like "*l'art brut*" (French for "raw art") have also been used. Still other people suggest that specific terms like "self-taught African Americans from the South" work best.

60 A period of serious interest in folk art began around 1970. At that time, both **collectors** and artists started attending local fairs, especially in the South. Word spread about a growing number of people who were making colorful objects out of the most surprising materials. This folk art soon began to appear in small museums and art galleries.

65 Folk art had always been there—the art world had just discovered its existence. This happened at a time of great change in the United States. The Civil Rights Movement, protests against the Vietnam War, and even rock 'n' roll music had helped change the cultural climate. Traditional thought about the arts was also changing. Music and art festivals inspired
70 interest in traditional folk ways of living.

In the middle to late 1980s, folk art experienced its greatest growth. Major museums held exhibitions. **Art dealers** began searching the South for new artists and works to display in their galleries. Books, conferences, and organizations were devoted to discussing and promoting folk art
75 throughout the country.

The most popular artist of this era—and one of the most famous folk artists in the last twenty-five years—was Howard Finster. Finster, who died in 2001, was a minister who produced thousands of original pieces. Finster's art has been on album covers for famous rock bands like REM.
80 On his land in Georgia, Finster built a "Paradise Garden." He continued with this project until his death. At the center of the garden is a 30-foot (9-meter) tower built of bicycle parts. Surrounding the tower is a concrete wall embedded with various items, including broken dolls, tools, clocks, and metal junk. Within the wall is his own church called "The World's
85 Folk Art Church." Finster said he put all these things together because he wanted to "mend a broken world."

Folk art has always been a part of American life. No matter what people call it, folk art has become very popular in the United States. Americans appreciate folk artists' unique ways of expressing themselves and their gifts
90 for bringing beauty into everyday life.

Read the passage again and answer the questions. Circle your answers.

MAIN IDEA

1. What is the main topic of this passage?
   A. how folk artists helped define American history
   B. the origin, development, and significance of American folk art
   C. the ways folk art influenced mainstream art
   D. the most famous folk artists in American history

DETAIL

2. Which group influenced the earliest American craft forms?
   A. Puritans who came over from England
   B. Spanish who settled California
   C. Native Americans who lived in the Southwest
   D. slaves from Africa

3. Folk art experienced its greatest growth in the 1980s when
   A. major museums held exhibits of folk art
   B. dealers began to search the South for talent
   C. art galleries displayed folk art
   D. all of the above

4. By definition, folk art
   A. comes from people who are separated from mainstream society
   B. is purchased primarily by large, mainstream museums
   C. generally is created by the children of the wealthy and educated
   D. all of the above

5. What two major events affected folk art's popularity in the 1970s?
   A. the Civil War and the end of slavery
   B. the birth and death of Howard Finster
   C. the Vietnam War and the Civil Rights Movement
   D. the beginning of rock 'n' roll and the band REM

6. Which of the following does **not** describe folk art?
   A. art school style
   B. natural feelings
   C. unusual materials
   D. tells a story

7. Howard Finster did which of the following?
   A. He painted a famous scene from the Civil War.
   B. He was in a famous rock band.
   C. He taught at a large university in the South.
   D. He created a large garden with a tower.

8. Which of the following would a folk artist be most likely to paint?
   A. a mountain in Japan
   B. people at a relative's funeral
   C. the Eiffel Tower in France
   D. a portrait of a movie star

INFERENCE

9. How did art dealers help folk artists?
   A. Art dealers taught folk artists new techniques.
   B. Buying and selling folk art created interest.
   C. Art dealers didn't buy folk art.
   D. Art dealers helped artists find materials.

10. Why is "self-taught" a good way to describe folk artists?
    A. It means that they are educated but in their own way.
    B. It shows that they could not pay for art school.
    C. It tells us that they didn't like their teachers in high school.
    D. It suggests that they think about themselves too much.

VOCABULARY REVIEW

WHICH MEANING?

From Chapter 1: *Thornton Dial: Folk Artist*

1. What does *canvas* mean in the following sentence?

   These included metal, wood, canvas, and sometimes, plastics.

   A. canvas *(noun)* a type of strong cloth
   B. canvas *(noun)* the floor of a boxing ring
   C. canvas *(verb)* to find out people's opinions about something

From Chapter 2: *The American South*

2. What does *block* mean in the following sentence?

   The Southern states tend to vote as a unified block.

   A. block *(noun)* a wooden building toy
   B. block *(noun)* a group
   C. block *(noun)* an area of land with streets on four sides

From Chapter 3: *American Folk Art*

3. What does *eye* mean in the following sentence?

   What makes a person an artist, though, is an eye for turning common objects into works with meaning.

   A. eye *(noun)* one of the two organs we see with
   B. eye *(noun)* the ability to see things in a special way
   C. eye *(noun)* the center of a large storm

WRONG WORD

One word in each group does not fit. Circle the word.

1. bright   colorful   humid   vivid
2. evolve   change   display   develop
3. craft   basketmaking   ceramics   sophisticated
4. hospitality   collage   sculpture   painting
5. contemporary   isolated   modern   new
6. collector   art dealer   gallery   headquarters

WORDS IN CONTEXT

Fill in the blanks with words from each box.

| formal | hospitality | humid | split | symbol |

1. My grandmother was known for her _____. She always had coffee and cake ready for guests.

2. That company's _____ is easy to recognize. They use it on all of their advertising.

3. His _____ education went only as far as the eighth grade.

4. The South wanted to _____ from the North. This was the cause of the Civil War.

5. I don't like hot, _____ weather. During the summer, I prefer to be in an air conditioned building.

| confident | contemporary | originated | pattern | phenomenal |

6. Several states have had _____ growth in recent years. Housing is less expensive, and jobs are available.

7. Do you prefer traditional or _____ furniture in your living room?

8. Her parents were _____ that she would succeed in life.

9. The artist used a red and blue _____ at the top of the bowl.

10. Several unique styles of folk art _____ in the South. One of these was pottery jugs that look like heads.

| displayed | extends | headquarters | sculptures | sophisticated |

11. The museum _____ Dial's work with the work of other folk artists.

12. The highway _____ from one side of the state to the other.

13. The artist came from a simple background. She wasn't terribly _____.

14. The museum plans to exhibit two large _____ by that artist.

15. Last year, the company moved its _____ to Atlanta. Employees love the new city.

WORD FAMILIES

Fill in the blanks with words from each box.

| isolate (noun) | isolation (noun) | isolated (adjective) |

1. The patient was put in _____ to avoid spreading the illness.

2. With no friends or family around, she felt _____.

| symbol *(noun)* | symbolize *(verb)* | symbolic *(adjective)* |

3. What do tigers _____ for Thornton Dial?

4. For Dial, tigers are _____ of African Americans.

| collection *(noun)* | collector *(noun)* | collect *(verb)* |

5. Do you _____ anything like stamps or coins?

6. She has an extensive _____ of folk art.

WRAP IT UP

DISCUSS THE THEME

Read these questions and discuss them with your partner.

1. Do you consider yourself an artistic person?

2. Have you ever made any of the following?
- a painting
- a drawing
- a sculpture
- a collage
- some unusual "thing" like those made by Thornton Dial or Howard Finster

3. Describe what you made. What materials did you use? Was your effort successful?

4. Have you ever taken or wanted to take art classes?

RESPOND IN WRITING

Look back at the unit and choose the passage you enjoyed the most. Read it again. Write a one-paragraph summary of the passage in your notebook.

What do you think is the most interesting thing about this passage, and why? Write a paragraph in your notebook.

U.S. HISTORY
THE HAWAIIAN ISLANDS

▲ The Hawaiian Islands

BEFORE YOU READ

Answer these questions.

1. Describe what you see in the image. Where is Hawaii in relation to the mainland of the United States?

2. What do you know about Hawaii? When did it become a part of the United States?

3. Have you ever visited Hawaii? Would you like to?

CHAPTER 1

Queen Lili'uokalani, 1838–1917

PREPARE TO READ

Discuss these questions.

1. Has the United States ever had a king or queen?

2. What kinds of things do kings and queens do?

WORD FOCUS

Match the words with their definitions.

A.

1. annex ___   **a.** a country ruled by a king or queen
2. ashore ___   **b.** an agreement in which both sides get part of what they want
3. compromise ___   **c.** enter a country with an army to attack it
4. invade ___   **d.** take control of another country or region
5. kingdom ___   **e.** onto the land from the sea

B.

1. monarchy ___   **a.** a tall, thin plant with a sweet sap
2. pardon ___   **b.** a government ruled by a king or queen
3. ruler ___   **c.** forgive someone officially and not give punishment
4. sugar cane ___   **d.** fighting between different countries or groups
5. war ___   **e.** the person who leads a country, usually a king or queen

SCAN

Guess if this is true or false. Circle *a* or *b*.

Sugar cane played an important role in Hawaii's history.

a. True   **b.** False

Scan the passage quickly to check your answer.

Queen Lili'uokalani: Hawaii's Queen

Hawaii is the name of a group of beautiful islands in the Pacific Ocean. Although the islands are far from the states that are on the North American continent, they are part of the United States. Hawaii became the 50th state in 1959, after many years as a U.S. territory. Hawaii has its own
5 unique history and culture. For example, before it became a U.S. territory, Hawaii was a **monarchy**. A monarchy is a country with a king or queen, not a president or prime minister.

The **kingdom** of Hawaii had many interesting **rulers**. King Kamehameha is the most famous of Hawaii's rulers, but he was not the last
10 monarch. The last ruler of Hawaii was a woman, Queen Lydia Lili'uokalani. She was the most loved and honored of the Hawaiian monarchs.

Princess Lydia

Princess Lydia Lili'uokalani was born in 1838 into a royal family. By this time, Hawaii and the United States were already doing a lot of business
15 together. Americans had a strong influence on the economy and culture of Hawaii. It was fashionable for Hawaiians to adopt the clothes and manners of the Americans. Families sent their children to special schools to learn Western languages and customs.

When Princess Lydia was just four years old, she started to attend the
20 Royal School. There, she learned English and the polite ways of American society. She traveled often, but she always remembered her Hawaiian culture and her native language.

Princess Lydia was married when she was 24 years old. Her husband became the governor of Oahu and Maui, two of Hawaii's eight large
25 islands. When she was 43, she made an important decision for Hawaii. At the time, her brother, King Kalakaua, was on a journey around the world. While he was gone, a terrible disease called smallpox hit the islands. It spread rapidly, and many Hawaiians died. Lydia decided that the epidemic was caused by workers who came from other countries to work in the
30 **sugar cane** fields. Sugar cane was a very profitable crop, but to protect her people, Lydia closed the ports to foreign ships. No products or people could come in, and no sugar cane could go out.

It was a very unpopular decision. It made life difficult for the sugar cane growers and for some of her people. But the princess stood by her decision.
35 She showed that the health of the Hawaiian people was more important than the money that sugar would bring. When the epidemic passed, her people were grateful for her strength.

Queen Lili'uokalani

Princess Lydia became queen of Hawaii in 1891, after her brother died.
40 Queen Lili'uokalani knew that Hawaii was changing. Hawaii's sugar cane crop was increasingly valuable. It was important to U.S. businesses and to people in Hawaii.

One year before she became queen, the Hawaiian government increased taxes on sugar. Sugar cane growers, most of them white businessmen, were
45 angry. They wanted a stronger relationship with the United States. They

continued

began to think that Hawaii's monarchy was hurting their business. They wanted a government that was friendlier to their business interests.

Queen Lili'uokalani could feel the power of the businessmen. Soon after she became queen, she tried to make a new constitution that would give 50 more power to the monarchy and to native Hawaiians. The businessmen didn't like this idea. They asked the U.S. government to send troops to **invade** Hawaii and take control.

On January 16, 1893, four boatloads of U.S. Marines came **ashore** in Honolulu. The Queen and her people stayed calm. The Royal Hawaiian band 55 even played a concert at the Hawaiian Hotel as the troops marched through the streets. Fortunately, the invasion didn't lead to **war**. Lydia, however, was forced to give up her throne, only three years after becoming queen.

A representative of the U.S. government, James H. Blount, arrived in Hawaii to try to arrange a **compromise** between the Americans and 60 Hawaiians. Blount and U.S. President Grover Cleveland wanted Hawaii to keep its monarchy, but they needed something in return. They offered Queen Lili'uokalani her crown back if she forgave and publicly **pardoned** the people who were against her. At first, she was angry and would not agree. After a month, she finally agreed to a pardon. But it was too late.

65 During that month, President Cleveland had asked the U.S. Congress what should be done. Many of the politicians were friends of the sugar growers. These politicians wanted to **annex** Hawaii as a territory of the United States. First, Hawaii became a republic on July 4, 1894. The former queen tried one last time to win back her kingdom. She went to 70 Washington in 1896 to talk to President Cleveland, but the time for this option had passed. In 1898, Hawaii became a U.S. territory. Hawaii was no longer a monarchy, and Lydia was no longer a queen.

The End of the Monarchy

The queen was now a private citizen, but she was still a queen to her 75 people. On her 60th birthday, many loyal subjects visited her at her home. They presented her with gifts and kneeled in her presence. As they left, they walked backwards out of the room so that they would not turn their backs to her. It was a symbolic gesture.

The ex-queen wrote a book, *Hawaii's Story by Hawaii's Queen*. The book 80 was very popular. It expresses her sadness over the changes that happened to her land and the end of the monarchy in Hawaii.

In 1917, Lydia Lili'uokalani died at the age of 79. A statue of her stands outside the state capitol building in Honolulu today. People still decorate the statue with flowers, a sign of their love for their queen.

85 Her memory lives on in other ways. During her life, Queen Lili'uokalani wrote more than 160 songs. Her most famous work is "Aloha Oe," which is a beautiful but sad song about two lovers who must separate. "Aloha Oe" is probably the most well-known Hawaiian song. In English, the song says,

Farewell to you, farewell to you.
90 O fragrance of one who dwells in the blue depths,
One fond embrace, until I return,
Until we meet again.

Read the passage again and answer the questions. Circle your answers.

MAIN IDEA
1. What is the main topic of the passage?
   A. fighting in early Hawaii
   B. the influence of the U.S. on Hawaii
   C. the last monarch in Hawaii
   D. the sugar cane business in Hawaii

DETAIL
2. Queen Lili'uokalani was born in
   A. 1838
   B. 1891
   C. 1917
   D. 1959

3. Why did Hawaiian families send their children to a special school?
   A. to learn how to grow sugar cane
   B. because the monarchy required it
   C. because it was fashionable
   D. to learn about Hawaiian culture and manners

4. Who was Queen Lili'uokalani's brother?
   A. King Kamehameha
   B. King Kalakaua
   C. James H. Blount
   D. Grover Cleveland

5. Queen Lili'uokalani wanted a new constitution
   A. to give the monarchy more power
   B. to give sugar cane growers more power
   C. to give the United States more power
   D. to put more taxes on sugar

6. Who was James H. Blount?
   A. a U.S. Marine
   B. the U.S. president
   C. a U.S. businessman
   D. a U.S. representative

7. In 1898, the United States
   A. annexed Hawaii as a territory
   B. started a monarchy in Hawaii
   C. sent troops to invade Hawaii
   D. made Hawaii an independent republic

8. Which of the following did Queen Lili'uokalani do?
   A. started growing sugar cane in Hawaii
   B. invited the United States to take over Hawaii
   C. wrote songs about Hawaii
   D. all of the above

INFERENCE
9. Why did Princess Lydia close the ports?
   A. because she wanted to contain the smallpox epidemic
   B. because she wanted to punish the sugar cane growers
   C. because she wanted to control the sugar cane crop
   D. because she wanted to increase the demand for sugar

10. Which of the following is true?
   A. Lili'uokalani hurt the sugar cane business in Hawaii.
   B. Lili'uokalani is a symbol of Hawaiian culture and history.
   C. Lili'uokalani was the first woman to travel outside Hawaii.
   D. Lili'uokalani wanted Hawaii to join the United States.

CHAPTER 2

◀ Kilauea erupting

PREPARE TO READ

Discuss these questions.

1. Why do you think that people like to visit Hawaii?

2. Would you like to see a volcano erupt? Why or why not?

WORD FOCUS

Match the words with their definitions.

A.
1. agriculture ___   **a.** a number of things in a line
2. chain ___   **b.** an object that is easily seen from a distance
3. climate ___   **c.** farming; the growing of plants or animals for food
4. harbor ___   **d.** a place on the coast where ships can stay safely
5. landmark ___   **e.** the normal weather conditions of a region

B.
1. lava ___   **a.** a mountain from which hot liquid rock and gas explode
2. mainland ___   **b.** wild birds and animals
3. plantation ___   **c.** hot liquid rock that comes out of a volcano
4. volcano ___   **d.** a large farm in a tropical climate
5. wildlife ___   **e.** the main part of a country, not including islands around it

SCAN

Guess if this is true or false. Circle *a* or *b*.

Hawaii traded sandalwood with China.

a. True   **b.** False

Scan the passage quickly to check your answer.

Hawaii: The 50th State

The 50th state of the United States is a group of islands in the Pacific Ocean. There are eight main islands and many small islands in the Hawaiian Islands **chain**. The large islands are, in order from northwest to southeast, Nihau, Kauai, Oahu, Molokai, Lanai, Kahoolawe, Maui, and the big island
5 of Hawaii. The eight stripes in Hawaii's flag represent these eight islands. Hawaii is located about 2,500 miles (4,000 km) west of the U.S. **mainland**, and it is a five-hour flight from California. Though the early Hawaiians traveled between islands by boat, most people today use small planes.

Geography

10 The Hawaiian Islands are volcanic islands. **Volcanoes** on the ocean floor erupted, and **lava** built up. Eventually, the mountains of lava grew above the water level, and the islands were formed. This process has been taking place over millions of years. It still continues, and both tourists and scientists travel to Hawaii to visit and study its active volcanoes.

15 Hawaii has a varied geography. Although it is known for its beaches, there are snow-covered mountains on the Big Island. Hawaii has a mild tropical **climate**. Many people say its climate is perfect. The islands have many unique geographical features, plants, and **wildlife**.

Oahu

20 Oahu is the island that most tourists visit. The main airport is there, and many hotels line the famous Waikiki Beach. The capital Honolulu is on Oahu. Honolulu has a wonderful natural **harbor**. This port was where many foreign ships arrived. The Hawaiian government charged a tax to each foreign ship. This tax, taken in either money or products, was an
25 important source of income for the kingdom.

Surfing has always been a popular sport in Hawaii. Early visitors wrote about seeing the islanders surfing on wooden boards. Some of these early surfboards are in the Bishop Museum on Oahu. Oahu is the site of many surfing competitions. Each winter, some of the largest waves in the world
30 hit Oahu, making it ideal for surfing.

Diamond Head is probably the most recognizable **landmark** in Hawaii. It is part of an extinct, or dead, volcano. It sits at the end of Waikiki Beach. British sailors gave it that name in the 1800s because it looks like a large diamond. Today, many people ride bicycles down the slope or hike to the
35 top to see the magnificent views.

Maui

The third-largest island, Maui, is known for its **agriculture**. Maui is a major producer of pineapple and sugar as well as beef cattle. Maui attracts tourists because of its natural beauty. It is also a favorite spot of whale watchers.

40 Kauai

Kauai is home to Waimea Canyon, which is called the Grand Canyon of the Pacific. Trails take hikers along the edge and down into the canyon. Tourists can also take a helicopter ride over the canyon.

continued

Hawaii

45 The big island of Hawaii has many miles of beaches as well as an active volcano, Kilauea. Kilauea has had continuous eruptions for over twenty years. Tourists can see fiery red lava flows forming new land. These lava flows make Hawaii the only state that is increasing in size.

On top of Mauna Kea, an inactive volcano, is an observatory with eleven
50 large telescopes. Astronomers from around the world come to this location to search the heavens. The location is a good one because it is at a high elevation and it is far away from city lights. Tourists can visit the site and look at the stars. The Big Island is also home to cattle ranches and coffee **plantations**.

Lanai

55 Lanai has many historical sites and old fishing villages that tourists like to visit. This island also has a site with rock carvings done by ancient Hawaiians.

Tourism makes up a large part of the economy. There are many hotels and tourist businesses on Oahu, Maui, Lanai, Kauai, and Hawaii. Hawaii is the only state that was once a kingdom with its own kings and queens.
60 In fact, the only palace in the United States is in Hawaii. The Iolani Palace on Oahu is a museum. There, visitors can see how the Hawaiian monarchs once lived.

Outside Influences

When missionaries arrived in Hawaii in 1820 to teach their religion, they
65 also brought the culture of the mainland United States. They established a written language for Hawaiian. They built churches and schools in the architectural style of New England. Many of these buildings still exist today. They look very different from the island-style houses and shops.

At the same time, trade with other nations increased. Hawaii traded
70 sandalwood in exchange for other goods. Sandalwood was highly valued in China and brought a good price. Both pineapple and sugar were planted on Hawaii and proved to be very profitable. However, these crops need a lot of people to harvest them, so workers from other countries came to work in the fields. Workers came from China, Japan, and Portuguese
75 Madeira and helped to create the multicultural mix that is Hawaii today.

From Kingdom to Statehood

Hawaii became an important trading partner with the United States. The United States bought sugar and pineapple from Hawaii and saw it as a safe harbor for its ships. People from the mainland built plantations.
80 The relationship between Hawaii and the United States was a good one. However, in 1893, a group of American businessmen decided to form a new government in Hawaii and remove Queen Lili'uokalani from power. U.S. sailors marched on the palace with guns and forced the queen to surrender. These businessmen then asked the U.S. government to make
85 Hawaii a territory. The United States needed a safe harbor in the Pacific, so in 1898 the U.S. Congress made Hawaii a U.S. territory.

On August 21, 1959, Hawaii became the 50th state. It was the last state to join the union. The climate, geography, and history of Hawaii are all uniquely different. From its monarchy to its volcanoes and beaches, this
90 island paradise is like no other state.

Read the passage again and answer the questions. Circle your answers.

MAIN IDEA

1. What is the main topic of this passage?
   A. surfing on Oahu
   B. the Hawaiian Islands
   C. Hawaii's people
   D. volcanoes on the Big Island

DETAIL

2. The missionaries who arrived in Hawaii
   A. were expert surfers
   B. marched on the palace with guns
   C. rode their bicycles on Diamond Head
   D. established a written language for Hawaiian

3. Hawaii became a state in
   A. 1820
   B. 1890
   C. 1959
   D. 1995

4. Which of the following is **not** true?
   A. The queen sold Hawaii to American businessmen.
   B. Hawaii's climate is good for farming.
   C. The land in Hawaii was formed by volcanoes.
   D. Islanders surfed before foreigners came to Hawaii.

5. What do the eight stripes on the Hawaiian flag represent?
   A. the eight main crops grown in Hawaii
   B. the eight languages spoken in Hawaii
   C. the eight main islands of Hawaii
   D. the eight founders of Hawaii

6. Honolulu, the capital of Hawaii, is on
   A. Oahu
   B. Lanai
   C. the big island of Hawaii
   D. Kauai

7. Which of these is produced on Maui?
   A. pineapple
   B. diamonds
   C. surfboards
   D. sandalwood

8. Hawaii is the only state in the U.S. that
   A. produces beef
   B. attracts tourists
   C. is increasing in size
   D. has surfing competitions

INFERENCE

9. Which of the following is probably true?
   A. Hawaiians did not like to eat beef or pineapple.
   B. There weren't enough Hawaiians to work on the plantations.
   C. Active lava flows are a good place to walk and ride bicycles.
   D. All of the architecture on the islands is the same.

10. Why is Hawaii so important to ships?
   A. It is the only land in the Pacific Ocean.
   B. Ships can get fuel there.
   C. Ships can find the islands easily.
   D. all of the above

CHAPTER 3

◀ An outrigger canoe

PREPARE TO READ

Discuss these questions.

1. Have you ever visited Hawaii? Would you like to visit? Why or why not?

2. How is Hawaii different from the place you live?

WORD FOCUS

Match the words with their definitions.

A.

1. canoe ___   **a.** sing a word or phrase many times
2. chant ___   **b.** a person who lives in a particular place
3. enforce ___   **c.** moving in a smooth or attractive way
4. graceful ___   **d.** a light, narrow boat
5. inhabitant ___   **e.** make sure that laws are obeyed

B.

1. legend ___   **a.** a religious or social custom that forbids certain actions
2. official ___   **b.** an action or ceremony usually repeated in the same way
3. ritual ___   **c.** approved by the government
4. stability ___   **d.** an old story that may or may not be true
5. taboo ___   **e.** the ability to remain in an upright or unchanged position

SCAN

Guess if this is true or false. Circle *a* or *b*.

Hawaii has four official languages.

a. True   **b.** False

Scan the passage quickly to check your answer.

Hawaiian Culture

The Polynesians settled the islands that we know today as Hawaii. It is believed that the first Polynesians arrived in Hawaii as early as the 5th century from the Marquesas Islands. Later groups arrived from Tahiti.

The Polynesians traveled the ocean in long **canoes**. Some of their
5 canoes were as long as 100 feet (30 m). Many were double or had outriggers, special parts on the sides, for **stability**. The Polynesians knew how to sail, swim, and fish very well. The travelers also carried seeds, plants, and small animals to use for food. They built their villages and planted taro, bananas, and coconuts. They also brought their culture, which
10 can be seen in the customs of the Hawaiian people.

Legends

The Polynesians brought their **legends**, or stories, with them. Legends about the gods and their interactions with each other and with humans are the basis of many stories and songs in these islands.

15 The two main gods were Ku, the god of war, and Lono, the god of peace and agriculture. War was an important part of Polynesian life, and Ku helped bring success in war. Lono was also the god of wind and rain. Rain was very important to an agricultural people like the Hawaiians. When Captain Cook first came to Hawaii, he was mistaken for the god
20 Lono. Some say this mistake was the reason the islanders welcomed Cook and his men.

The volcano goddess Pele could make volcanoes explode in a show of fire. The Polynesians respected the force of lava and believed that this goddess controlled the flow of lava and, therefore, the lives of the
25 **inhabitants** of these islands.

The religious men, or *kahunas,* carved wooden statues to represent their gods and goddesses. There was a different statue for each god. The statues were often tall. The Hawaiians believed that the statues had power and could **enforce** the rules known as *kapus.*

30 ## *Kapus* or Forbidden Actions

A system of *kapus,* forbidden actions, existed. Some actions were forbidden by the gods and goddesses. Other actions were not allowed according to Hawaiian society. As a result, a number of actions were forbidden to ancient Hawaiians. Many of the rules related to the interactions of men
35 and women. Many were specifically aimed at women. Women, for example, were not allowed to eat bananas, even though there were many bananas on the islands. Only high-ranking men could eat bananas. If a woman or a young girl was seen eating a banana, she was punished. Women were also not allowed to eat in the same places as men. Rank, however, was passed
40 on through the mother's line.

Hula Dances

Hula is a form of **chant** and dance in the Hawaiian Islands. Music accompanies the chanting. Hula dancers perform in a style that is based on many ancient **rituals**. Each hula dance tells a story. Most Hawaiians can

continued

45 understand the story by watching the **graceful** movement of the dancers'
fingers and bodies.

One legend says that Laka, the goddess of the hula dance, began the
dance on the island of Molokai. A festival for this event is still celebrated
every May. Before the Europeans came to Hawaii, hula was closely tied
50 to religious practices. Dances accompanied most important ceremonies.
Today, hula dances are performed both in rituals and for tourists. It is the
modern form of hula that most tourists see at resorts.

Food Rituals: *Luaus*

A *luau* is a big outdoor feast with an interesting history. In ancient Hawaii,
55 women and men ate their meals separately. Women and men who were not
part of the ruling class were forbidden to eat certain foods. This changed in
1819 when King Kamehameha II ended a number of traditional practices.
To show that he was serious about this change, the king ate with women
at a large feast. This showed the Hawaiian people that the old **taboos** were
60 gone. The favorite dish at this feast is what gave the luau its name. Chicken
was covered with tender leaves of the taro plant and baked in coconut milk.
This dish was called *luau.*

At a typical luau, the feast was eaten on the floor. Mats were rolled
out on the floor and plates of food were set on the mats. All of the food
65 was eaten with the fingers. A king named Kalakaua, known as the "Merry
Monarch," invited over 1,500 guests to a luau for his 50th birthday.

Leis or Flower Necklaces

Hawaii is full of plants and flowers. An old Hawaiian custom that is still
practiced today is the giving of a *lei,* a string of flowers. A *lei* is given to
70 a visitor or to a person returning home. It is worn like a necklace and is
made from fresh flowers. Plumeria or orchids are typical flowers used to
make leis. Plumeria has a pleasant, sweet smell.

Language

Today Hawaii has two **official** languages: Hawaiian and English. Most
75 Hawaiians speak English and use many Hawaiian words in their daily
lives. Hawaiian was only a spoken language before the missionaries came
to Hawaii. They developed the first written form of Hawaiian in the early
19th century.

The Hawaiian alphabet consists of only 12 letters: five vowels (a, e, i, o, u)
80 and seven consonants (h, k, l, m, n, p, w). Every syllable ends in a vowel,
and every vowel is pronounced. This leads to some very long names and
words. For example, there is a fish whose name is "humuhumununkunu
kuapua'a." Some Hawaiian words are familiar to Americans in the other
49 states. These include words like *luau* (a big outdoor party), *aloha* (a
85 greeting or farewell), and *ukulele* (a very small guitar). Some Americans
refer to the boss as "the big kahuna." A *kahuna* was a religious man.

While Hawaiian culture has changed in the last 250 years, it has also
become known around the world. Many people want to visit these islands
to eat at a luau, wear a lei of beautiful flowers, and watch the graceful hula
90 dancers.

Read the passage again and answer the questions. Circle your answers.

MAIN IDEA

1. What is the main topic of this passage?
   A. what women were allowed to eat at luaus
   B. why Hawaiians give leis
   C. the movements in a hula dance
   D. the culture of Hawaii

DETAIL

2. Pele was known as the goddess of
   A. rain
   B. wind
   C. dance
   D. volcanoes

3. The word *luau* was originally the name of
   A. a chant used in hula dancing
   B. a flower used in making leis
   C. a chicken dish
   D. a goddess

4. The forbidden actions were called
   A. kapus
   B. leis
   C. alohas
   D. luaus

5. Which of the following is one of the official languages of Hawaii?
   A. Lono
   B. English
   C. Polynesian
   D. Pele

6. Why did the islanders welcome Captain Cook and his men?
   A. They thought Cook was a god.
   B. They heard about Cook in legends.
   C. Cook came to the islands in long canoes.
   D. Cook made volcanoes explode in a show of fire.

7. Religious men made tall wooden statues of
   A. Captain Cook and his men
   B. Polynesians
   C. hula dancers
   D. gods and goddesses

8. A Hawaiian *lei* is made of what?
   A. lava
   B. carved wood
   C. flowers
   D. 12 letters

INFERENCE

9. Which of the following is true?
   A. Polynesian boats were only used on lakes and rivers.
   B. The Polynesians explored the Pacific Islands.
   C. The Polynesians did not know about farming.
   D. all of the above

10. What can we say about the Hawaiian gods?
    A. Hawaiians believed in their power.
    B. The people did not believe in them.
    C. All of the Hawaiian gods were males.
    D. The people called the gods *kahunas*.

VOCABULARY REVIEW

WHICH MEANING?

From Chapter 1: *Queen Lili'uokalani: Hawaii's Queen*

1. What does *crown* mean in the following sentence?

> They offered Queen Lili'uokalani her crown back if she forgave and publicly pardoned the people who were against her.

   A. crown *(noun)* the round ornament worn on the head to symbolize power
   B. crown *(noun)* the top of the head; the head
   C. crown *(noun)* in some countries, the name for money

From Chapter 2: *Hawaii: The 50th State*

2. What does *line* mean in the following sentence?

> The main airport is there, and many hotels line the famous Waikiki Beach.

   A. line *(verb)* to cover an inside surface with a different material
   B. line *(verb)* to make a row
   C. line *(noun)* a mark on the side of a playing field

From Chapter 3: *Hawaiian Culture*

3. What does *resort* mean in the following sentence?

> It is the modern form of hula that most tourists see at resorts.

   A. resort *(noun)* a place where people go on vacation
   B. resort *(noun)* the last option
   C. resort *(verb)* to do something unpleasant because you have no choice

WRONG WORD

One word in each group does not fit. Circle the word.

1. luau	legend	feast	party
2. landmark	queen	ruler	monarch
3. battle	fight	war	chant
4. tourist	foreigner	inhabitant	visitor
5. forbidden	graceful	wrong	illegal
6. compromise	tradition	custom	ritual

WORDS IN CONTEXT

Fill in the blanks with words from each box.

ashore	mainland	plantations	volcano	war

1. The passengers had to swim _____ after the boat sank.
2. It took us five hours to fly from San Francisco on the _____ to Honolulu.
3. Though there was a lot of tension, Hawaii never went to _____ with the United States.
4. Large sugar _____ covered much of the island.
5. The _____ erupted and threw out hot gas and lava.

chain	invaded	legend	official	wildlife

6. The _____ was a nice story, but it was not true.
7. The United States _____ Hawaii because its business interests were at risk.
8. Birds make up most of Hawaii's _____. It is difficult for most other animals to travel from island to island.
9. English and Hawaiian are the two _____ languages in Hawaii.
10. Hawaii is a _____ of volcanic islands. Some of the islands are quite small.

canoes	graceful	lava	monarchy	rituals

11. Most ceremonies include _____ that have special meaning.
12. A king or a queen rules in a _____.
13. _____ hula dancers entertain tourists at many of the resorts.
14. The Polynesians rode their _____ between the islands.
15. Hot _____ flows out of volcanoes during an eruption.

WORD FAMILIES

Fill in the blanks with words from each box.

invasion *(noun)*	invader *(noun)*	invade *(verb)*

1. The sugar cane growers wanted the United States to _____ Hawaii and end the monarchy.
2. The _____ took place as the band played at the main hotel.

| inhabitant *(noun)* | inhabit *(verb)* | inhabited *(adjective)* |

3. This house doesn't look _____. Do you think anyone lives here?

4. The guide told me that dangerous animals _____ this forest. We should be careful.

| stability *(noun)* | stabilize *(verb)* | stable *(adjective)* |

5. This chair isn't very _____. It feels like it's going to break.

6. The government needs to _____ the economy.

WRAP IT UP

DISCUSS THE THEME

Read these questions and discuss them with your partner.

1. What place have you always dreamed of visiting? Why?

2. What things would you do if you visited this place?

3. What would you tell people to visit in your area?

4. What are some interesting customs in your area?

RESPOND IN WRITING

Look back at the unit and choose the passage you enjoyed the most. Read it again. Write a one-paragraph summary of the passage in your notebook.

What do you think is the most interesting thing about this passage, and why? Write a paragraph in your notebook.

BUSINESS
TECHNOLOGY

▲ Cars on an assembly line

Answer these questions.

1. What are the different parts of a car? Name as many as you can.

2. How are cars made today?

3. Which do you think is safer: a car made by people or a car made by robots? Why?

CHAPTER 1

Henry Ford, 1863–1947, at the wheel of a Model T with Thomas Edison in the rear seat

PREPARE TO READ

Discuss these questions.

1. What do you know about the first cars?

2. How do autoworkers put a car together? What do they probably do first? What do they probably do last?

WORD FOCUS

Match the words with their definitions.

A.
1. conveyor belt ___
2. engine ___
3. maintain ___
4. manufacturer ___
5. ordinary ___

a. the part of a machine that changes energy into movement
b. a company that makes something using machines
c. normal; not unusual
d. a moving surface that carries things from one place to another
e. keep something in good condition

B.
1. plant ___
2. shift ___
3. station ___
4. suburb ___
5. tough ___

a. a place outside the center of a city where people live
b. a large factory
c. strong; difficult to beat
d. a division of the workday
e. a place within a factory where one particular job is done

SCAN

Guess if this is true or false. Circle *a* or *b*.

Henry Ford made his employees work long hours.

a. True   **b.** False

Scan the passage quickly to check your answer.

Henry Ford: Ideas that Changed a Nation

Can you imagine a world without cars? Most adults in the United States and in many other countries have a car, but that wasn't always true. When cars were first invented, they were very expensive. Only wealthy people could afford to buy them. Henry Ford changed that when he developed a
5 way to make cars for much less money. **Ordinary** families could afford to buy a car. Ford sold millions of cars all over the world, and the company he founded is still one of the world's major automobile **manufacturers**.

Henry Ford was born in 1863 on a farm in Dearborn, Michigan. He never liked farm work. He preferred to work with machines and repair
10 small **engines**. When he was 16 years old, he moved to Detroit. In Detroit, Ford worked with electric engines, but he was most interested in gasoline-powered engines. He built one at his kitchen table, just to see how it worked.

In 1896, Ford built his first automobile—the Quadricycle. The wheels
15 looked like bicycle wheels. There was no steering wheel. It could go forward but not backward. It had many problems, but it worked! He wanted to build another car, a better car.

Henry Ford was not the first car manufacturer in the United States, or the only one. Two brothers, Charles and Frank Duryea, built a car in
20 Springfield, Massachusetts, in 1893. Then a man named Ransome Eli Olds opened an automobile factory in Detroit in 1901. Olds used a type of assembly line in his factory. Workers moved the body of a car from one **station** in the factory to the next. At every station, workers added parts to the car until they assembled the whole car. One car usually took almost
25 two days to assemble. In the year 1902, Olds built only 2,500 cars.

At first, Ford wasn't as successful as Olds. Ford needed to find a way to assemble his cars faster. One day, he visited a meat-packing **plant** in Chicago. He saw the meat move through the plant on **conveyor belts**. This gave him an idea: his assembly line could have a series of conveyor
30 belts for the car parts. This would make the line faster.

The Ford Motor Company opened in 1903. Ford promised he would build a car that most Americans could afford and enjoy. Five years later, two of his designers developed the Model T, or "Tin Lizzie." The price was just $950. This was a good price, but Ford wanted to find ways to make his
35 cars even less expensive.

By 1914, Ford could make a Model T in 93 minutes—about eight times faster than Olds. Americans loved the Model T. It was cheap, easy to drive, and easy to **maintain**. By 1918, half of all the cars in the United States were Model Ts. Ford didn't need to spend much money on advertising his
40 Model T. Everyone seemed to own a Model T or knew someone who did.

Henry Ford was also a good employer. Ford paid his workers five dollars a day, about twice the normal rate. Ford also cut the workday from nine to eight hours. This made it possible to have three equal **shifts** of workers. The factory then began to make cars 24 hours a day. This saved money,
45 and Ford lowered the price of a Model T to $280.

continued

Soon Ford opened automobile factories in other countries. He opened his first plant in Canada, just across the river from Detroit, in 1904. He opened plants in England in 1911, in Brazil in 1919, and in Germany and Australia in 1925. The Model T became popular all over the world.

50　　Another reason for Ford's success was his car parts. Before he developed his assembly line, Ford had bought car parts from other places and had brought them to his factory. Ford decided to make his own parts right at the factory. Ford purchased iron mines, coal mines, and a rubber plantation in Brazil. The company bought its own ships and its own

55 railroad company to bring materials to the giant factory.

Ford was proud of his Model T. In 1909, two of his Model Ts were in a 3,000-mile (4,800 km) race across the United States. They competed against cars that were far more expensive. One of the Model Ts won the race, and the other finished third. A driver in a modified Model T finished

60 fifth in the 1923 Indianapolis 500 motor race. A Model T was also the first to cross the United States on the Lincoln Highway. In 1926, another Model T set a record by crossing the United States in just five days.

Ford made the Model T for 20 years with very few changes. In total, he built more than 15 million of them. When Ford began to make cars

65 in 1903, he was one of 88 automobile manufacturers in the United States. In the 1920s, there were fewer competitors, but they were much **tougher**. By 1927, other automobile manufacturers started to make their own affordable cars, so the Model T was no longer special. Ford stopped making the Model T and started to work on other models.

70　　Henry Ford and his Model T changed the way people in the United States lived. Having a car gave people much more freedom. People didn't have to live in crowded, dirty cities to be close to their jobs. They could drive to their jobs. As a result, many people built houses on the edge of the city. These housing developments were the first **suburbs**.

75　　With so many cars, the United States needed more and better roads. Highways became wider and longer. In the 1950s, the federal government started to build the interstate highway system to meet the needs of drivers. This network of roadways connects cities and states.

Henry Ford died in 1947. Today, his Ford Motor Company makes

80 many different models of vehicles, even race cars. It is an international company with hundreds of thousands of employees, but it still uses Henry Ford's simple signature as its logo, or symbol. In many ways his simple yet innovative ideas shaped an entire industry.

Read the passage again and answer the questions. Circle your answers.

MAIN IDEA

1. What is the main topic of the passage?
   A. one man's effect on auto manufacturing
   B. the Model T
   C. early automakers
   D. the effect of cars on cities in the U.S.

DETAIL

2. What did Henry Ford do in Detroit?
   A. He went to college.
   B. He worked on a farm.
   C. He built bicycles.
   D. He worked with engines.

3. What was the name of the first automobile Henry Ford built?
   A. the Olds
   B. the Duryea
   C. the Quadricycle
   D. the Springfield

4. Where did Henry Ford get the idea to use conveyor belts in his factory?
   A. from Ransome Eli Olds
   B. from a meat-packing plant
   C. from bicycle wheels
   D. from two of his designers

5. How much did the first Model T cost?
   A. $93
   B. $280
   C. $950
   D. $2,500

6. By 1914, the Ford factory could make a Model T in
   A. 24 minutes
   B. 93 minutes
   C. 280 minutes
   D. 950 minutes

7. How much did Henry Ford pay his workers?
   A. twice the normal rate
   B. $8 a day
   C. $24 a day
   D. $280 a week

8. In total, how many Model T cars did the Ford Motor Company build?
   A. 88
   B. 500
   C. 3,000
   D. 15 million

INFERENCE

9. Why did Henry Ford shorten the workday to 8 hours?
   A. so workers could go home to the suburbs faster
   B. to lower the price of a Model T to $950
   C. to divide the workday into three equal shifts
   D. so his workers could earn $5 a day

10. How did the Model T change life in the U.S.?
    A. It made the automobile the most common form of transportation.
    B. It cost people less money to buy than other types of cars.
    C. It made the average workday eight hours long for most workers.
    D. It made the roads in the interstate highway system wider and longer.

CHAPTER 2

Detroit, Michigan

PREPARE TO READ

Discuss these questions.

1. Which American cities or states are famous for auto manufacturing?

2. What are some good things and bad things about a city with only one major industry?

WORD FOCUS

Match the words with their definitions.

A.

1. arsenal ___   **a.** a passenger vehicle pulled by horses
2. carriage ___   **b.** an economic need
3. clash ___   **c.** a place where weapons are made or stored
4. demand ___   **d.** pay someone to do work
5. employ ___   **e.** a fight or serious disagreement

B.

1. heritage ___   **a.** financial success
2. label ___   **b.** the pay you receive for work; salary
3. obvious ___   **c.** a music company and its name
4. prosperity ___   **d.** easily seen or understood; clear
5. wages ___   **e.** the traditions of a place that make it special

SCAN

Guess if this is true or false. Circle *a* or *b*.

Detroit had the first superhighway.

a. True   **b.** False

Scan the passage quickly to check your answer.

Detroit: The Motor City

Many big cities in the United States have nicknames. New York is "The Big Apple." Chicago is "The Windy City." Detroit is "The Motor City." Detroit got this nickname because it has been the home of the automobile industry in the United States for 100 years.

5   Detroit was settled many years before cars were invented. In 1701, a French explorer named Sieur Antoine de la Mothe Cadillac started the town. One of the most famous types of American cars is named the Cadillac in his honor. Cadillac called the new settlement "Ville d'Etroit." Over time, the name changed to just "Detroit." Detroit became a city in 10 the early 1800s. It was the first capital of the state of Michigan. Many people moved from Europe to Detroit to work in factories that made ships and stoves. They also made **carriages**. In the late 1800s, inventors developed the first automobiles, or "horseless carriages." Detroit was the **obvious** place to build them.

15   Many auto factories soon opened in Detroit. Then Henry Ford perfected the assembly line—a way to make many cars quickly and sell them cheaply. His "Model T" car was very popular, and he needed many workers to keep up with **demand**. More and more people moved to Detroit. The city's population doubled between 1830 and 1900. From 1910 to 1930, more 20 than one million more people moved to Detroit. It was the fourth largest city in the United States.

   General Motors and Chrysler—two other automakers—also chose Detroit as their headquarters in the early 20th century. The "Big Three" automakers **employed** thousands of workers and turned Detroit into "The 25 Motor City."

   Detroit's nickname was perfect. In 1909, Detroit became the first city in the United States to have roads paved with concrete. In 1918, a Detroit man named William Potts thought of a way to manage traffic. Potts took some wire and some red, yellow, and green railroad lights. He connected 30 the wire and the lights to an electric control at the corner of two streets. It was the first four-way, three-color traffic light in the world.

   The first "superhighway" in the United States was built in Detroit. In 1923, workers constructed an eight-lane road with a wide median in the center. The median divided traffic into four lanes going in each 35 direction. In 1929, Detroit's Ambassador Bridge over the Detroit River was the longest bridge in the world. In 1930, Detroit built the world's first international underwater car tunnel. It connected Detroit with Windsor, Ontario, Canada.

   Detroit was soon an exciting city and a wonderful place to visit. It had a 40 great streetcar system. There were many fine hotels and shops. There was a lot to see and do, including sports and concerts. Many African Americans from the southern United States moved to Detroit in the early 1900s to work in the auto factories. They brought all the aspects of their culture, including jazz music.

continued

45 The heart of Detroit's **prosperity** was the auto industry. Many workers believed that the car companies had too much power. These workers thought that the companies should pay them better **wages** and improve their working conditions. The workers wanted to unite and speak to the owners with one voice. The United Automobile Workers union was formed

50 in Detroit in 1935 to represent the autoworkers. Sometimes, the workers and companies disagreed. There were some violent **clashes**, but the city and the auto industry continued to grow.

The world soon found out that Detroit was not just a place to build cars. The United States needed airplanes during World War II. Henry Ford

55 used his famous assembly line to build thousands of airplanes. Because many of the men had gone to war, the workers in the factories were mostly women. Thousands of people moved to Detroit to work in factories that made things needed for the war. The city was proud to be called "The **Arsenal** of Democracy."

60 Detroit began to change after World War II. The city got bigger, and people moved into the suburbs. People needed faster ways to get to work in the city. The city built wide, smooth roads called expressways. On an expressway, people can drive fast and they don't have to stop. It was easy to go from one place to another on Detroit's expressways. Soon, most major

65 cities had expressways like Detroit's.

Over time, the giant factories in Detroit built fewer cars. Americans began to buy cars made in Germany and Japan. Plants opened in other places in the United States. More and more people started to move away to other cities or into the suburbs. The population of the city began to

70 decline. Many hotels and shops closed. The streetcars disappeared.

But the African American community stayed in Detroit. The city was still a good place to make and listen to music, especially jazz. In the 1960s, a man named Berry Gordy opened a record store and later a club where Detroit's best musicians played. Gordy wrote music and helped musicians

75 make records. Gordy decided to start his own record **label**. He needed a name for it. He decided to shorten Detroit's nickname "Motor City" and call his label "Motown." Major artists including Diana Ross, Stevie Wonder, and Marvin Gaye all began recording music on the Motown label. The Motor City no longer made as many cars, but Motown made one "hit

80 record" after another. Motown's music was popular all over the United States. It gave people from Detroit a reason to be proud of their city during hard times.

Today, Detroit still has problems. The population of the city is less than half what it was in 1950. But Detroit is trying to build itself up again. The

85 Fox Theater, which opened in 1928, is open again. There is a new baseball stadium in downtown Detroit. The Detroit Lions football team moved from a stadium in the suburbs to a downtown stadium. Detroit's **heritage** as "The Motor City" will last as long as there are cars.

Read the passage again and answer the questions. Circle your answers.

MAIN IDEA

1. What is the main topic of the passage?
   A. the history of the city of Detroit
   B. the history of the automobile industry
   C. the prosperity of Detroit
   D. the music industry in Detroit

DETAIL

2. Who started the town of Detroit?
   A. Cadillac
   B. Ville d'Etroit
   C. Henry Ford
   D. the "Big Three" automakers

3. Detroit was the obvious place to build cars because
   A. it was located on a large lake
   B. it had a long history of car manufacturing
   C. the carriage industry was already there
   D. it was the first capital of the state of Michigan

4. Which companies were known as the "Big Three" automakers?
   A. Ford, General Motors, and Chrysler
   B. General Motors, Chrysler, and Detroit
   C. Cadillac, General Motors, and Chrysler
   D. Cadillac, Ford, and Detroit

5. What was William Potts' idea for managing traffic?
   A. concrete roads
   B. colored traffic lights
   C. an eight-lane superhighway
   D. an underwater car tunnel

6. During World War II, many automobile factories also made
   A. clothing
   B. records
   C. expressways
   D. airplanes

7. How did Detroit change after World War II?
   A. The city started to use traffic lights.
   B. Many people moved to the suburbs.
   C. The population doubled.
   D. all of the above

8. Barry Gordy named his record label "Motown" in honor of
   A. Diana Ross
   B. African Americans
   C. the automobile industry
   D. Detroit

INFERENCE

9. How did Detroit become the fourth largest city in the U.S. by 1930?
   A. Many people went there to buy cars.
   B. Many people went there to work in car factories.
   C. Ford built airplanes in his factories during World War II.
   D. Musicians came there to make records on the Motown label.

10. What was the biggest reason for Detroit's economic problems?
    A. Car factories changed to airplane factories.
    B. The auto industry declined.
    C. Motown Records became less popular in the 1980s.
    D. The people moved to Canada.

CHAPTER 3

Robots on an auto assembly line

PREPARE TO READ

Discuss these questions.

1. Have you ever seen a robot? What did it do?
2. What types of jobs will robots of the future do?

WORD FOCUS

Match the words with their definitions.

A.

1. advantage ___   **a.** cause a vehicle to have an accident
2. attach ___   **b.** a piece of equipment for a particular purpose
3. crash ___   **c.** connect something to another thing
4. device ___   **d.** something that can help you or bring a good result
5. dummy ___   **e.** a model of a human body

B.

1. replace ___   **a.** the state of not being in danger
2. robot ___   **b.** use high heat to join pieces of metal
3. safety ___   **c.** someone who agrees to do something without being forced
4. volunteer ___   **d.** take the place of someone or something
5. weld ___   **e.** a machine that can move like a human

SCAN

Guess if this is true or false. Circle *a* or *b*.

In a car factory, robots can do anything a person can do.

a. True   **b.** False

Scan the passage quickly to check your answer.

Robots and Crash-Test Dummies

Henry Ford's ideas changed auto manufacturing forever. Two innovative types of technology have continued to transform the auto industry: **robots** and crash-test **dummies**. Robots have dramatically changed the assembly line process by taking over routine jobs that were previously done by
5 humans. Crash-test dummies have given manufacturers a way to test automobile **safety**.

Robots

Robots are amazing machines. They can be programmed to copy people's basic actions and movements. They can push, pull, lift, turn, and bend.
10 Robots can be programmed to do almost any kind of work. On a factory assembly line, robots can often do the work of many men and women. Robots have cost some people their jobs, but there are **advantages** to using robots.

In the early days of the auto industry, people put cars together by hand
15 on an assembly line. The body of a car moved on a conveyor belt from one station to the next until the car was finished. Autoworkers were proud of the cars that they built, but it wasn't easy to work on an assembly line. A person on an assembly line stood in one place. Henry Ford's assembly lines saved time and money, but often workers felt like they were machines, too.
20 The workers put the same part on one car after another for eight hours a day, five days a week. The work was neither fun nor challenging. Over time, workers got tired of it. They thought about other things and sometimes stopped paying attention to their work.

Workers needed to take a break and go on vacation. Workers got sick.
25 Every person did his or her job a little differently from other people. One worker might **attach** a part to a car tighter than another worker. No two cars were exactly the same. This sometimes caused problems and accidents. Automakers needed to find a way to make sure that their cars were safe and well made.

30 The first simple electronic computers appeared just after World War II. At about the same time, a man named George Devol invented a **device** that could control a machine so that the machine would do the same task repeatedly. Devol designed the first programmable robot in 1954. Devol and a man named Joseph F. Engelberger decided robots could save
35 companies time and money, so they started their own company, Universal Automation.

In 1961, a General Motors factory in New Jersey was the first to use a robot to put together cars. The robot was called Unimate. It lifted pieces of hot metal from a machine and put them into stacks. This job was neither
40 fun nor challenging, but Unimate didn't care. Unimate also didn't get sick or need to go on vacation. Unimate only worked, doing the same job exactly the same way over and over again. Not long afterward, robots were being used in automobile factories around the world. The new field of robotics had arrived in the auto industry.

45 The first robots didn't look like people at all. Robots in factories still don't look like people. They look like machines. They usually have one

continued

arm. That arm does all the work, whether it is **welding** two pieces of metal or painting a car part with a sprayer. A robot completes a task exactly the same way every time, something a human cannot do.

50   Although it is true that robots have **replaced** some human workers, humans haven't disappeared from the assembly line. Now the human workers move along the line doing more challenging tasks. Highly trained technical people also work day and night to keep the robots functioning properly.

55 **Crash-Test Dummies**

Cars make life easier, but from the first moment they appeared on the road, they have also made life more dangerous. From the beginning, automakers have looked for ways to make cars safer. Automakers had new ideas and inventions to improve safety, but manufacturers needed ways to
60 test their ideas before putting them into cars.

In the past, automakers **crashed** cars on test tracks to study what happened during an accident. Automakers had plenty of cars to crash, but they needed people, too. They needed to know if their safety devices really protected people in an accident.

65   At first, people **volunteered** to ride in the cars. Testers only crashed the cars lightly, but the volunteers still got hurt. That was too dangerous. Then the testers tried another method. They used dead bodies. This gave them some information, but not enough. They tried using live pigs, but that didn't work either. They needed to know what happens to a living person
70 in a crash.

In 1949, the United States Air Force built a dummy called "Sierra Sam" for rocket tests. Sam was the same height and weight as a man. The people who tested automobiles decided to use Sam for their tests, too. Could a dummy really show them what happens to a live person in a car accident?
75 The answer was yes!

Soon, automakers developed crash-test dummies of all sizes. Researchers needed to know what happened to women and to small children in an accident, not just men. The results led to safer cars in the 1950s. General Motors' crash-test dummies helped them develop better seat belts and air
80 bags in the 1970s.

Crashing an automobile has become a science. Today's crash-test dummies are very sophisticated. They are made to be exactly like people. Their body parts react to a crash the way a person's body parts would. These new dummies contain many instruments to measure the effects of a
85 crash and record the information for scientists.

Crash-test dummies have even become an easily recognizable part of modern culture. They have appeared in television ads. In addition, a 1990s rock-and-roll band from Canada had the name The Crash Test Dummies!

Robots and crash-test dummies have helped automakers build better,
90 cheaper, and safer cars. Unskilled jobs were lost as robots came into use, but new highly skilled technical jobs were created. The use of increasingly sophisticated crash-test dummies has helped prevent serious injury and has saved countless lives.

Read the passage again and answer the questions. Circle your answers.

MAIN IDEA
1. What is the main topic of the passage?
   A. crash-test dummies
   B. automobile safety devices
   C. new technology in the auto industry
   D. robots of the future

DETAIL
2. What can robots do?
   A. copy the actions and movements of people
   B. make decisions about automobile safety
   C. create new ways to solve safety problems
   D. choose the best way to put a car together

3. Why did workers not like to work on an assembly line?
   A. because the robots took their jobs away
   B. because they were proud of the cars they made
   C. because they did the same job over and over again
   D. because assembly lines save time and money

4. What was the name of the first robot in a car factory?
   A. George Devol
   B. Unimate
   C. Sierra Sam
   D. General Motors

5. Where were robots first used to build cars?
   A. in Canada
   B. in the Universal Automation Company
   C. at a General Motors factory in New Jersey
   D. in automobile factories around the world

6. To test safety devices today, automakers use
   A. living volunteers
   B. dead bodies
   C. living animals
   D. crash-test dummies

7. Cars have made life easier, but they have also made life
   A. more intelligent
   B. more dangerous
   C. safer
   D. longer

8. In the 1970s, what did crash-test dummies help automakers develop?
   A. better rocket tests
   B. better seat belts and air bags
   C. more body parts
   D. more sophisticated instruments

INFERENCE
9. What do crash-test dummies teach automakers?
   A. how people feel about car crashes
   B. the cheapest way to build cars
   C. what happens to people in a car crash
   D. when to use seat belts and when not to use them

10. Which of the following statements is true?
   A. There are more unskilled employees in auto manufacturing today.
   B. Robots were first used by the military to test the effects of space.
   C. Autoworkers hate robots and want them all to go away.
   D. It is better to use dummies than people to test cars.

VOCABULARY REVIEW

WHICH MEANING?

From Chapter 1: *Henry Ford: Ideas that Changed a Nation*

1. What does *edge* mean in this context?

> As a result, many people built houses on the edge of the city.

A. edge *(verb)* to move slowly and carefully across something
B. edge *(noun)* the place where something ends
C. edge *(noun)* a slight advantage over something or someone

From Chapter 2: *Detroit: The Motor City*

2. What does *heart* mean in this context?

> The heart of Detroit's prosperity was the auto industry.

A. heart *(noun)* the organ inside the chest that controls blood circulation
B. heart *(noun)* dedication to and enthusiasm about something
C. heart *(noun)* the central or most important part of something

From Chapter 3: *Robots and Crash-Test Dummies*

3. What does *body* mean in this context?

> The body of a car moved on a conveyor belt from one station to the next until the car was finished.

A. body *(noun)* a group acting in an official way
B. body *(noun)* the main part of something
C. body *(noun)* a dead human or animal

WRONG WORD

One word in each group does not fit. Circle the word.

1. tool	device	instrument	prosperity
2. special	ordinary	uncommon	unusual
3. headquarters	main office	heritage	center
4. manager	technician	dummy	employee
5. attach	weld	join	crash
6. obvious	sophisticated	complicated	advanced

WORDS IN CONTEXT

Fill in the blanks with words from each box.

conveyor belt	replace	maintain	volunteers	wages

1. Some people worry that robots will _____ human workers.

2. Products or parts of products usually move through a factory on a _____ .

3. People exercise to _____ good health and physical fitness.

4. Auto workers in the 1960s wanted higher _____ and better working conditions.

5. The manager asked for _____ to stay after work to finish the project.

demand	label	plants	shift	sophisticated

6. The Model T was extremely popular. Workers had problems meeting the _____ for the product.

7. Many of the most popular musicians in the 1960s recorded their music on the Motown _____ .

8. The first cars were not very _____ , but cars today are extremely complicated.

9. Some of Ford's employees worked the night _____ . They worked during the eight hours that other people slept.

10. Three of the biggest automobile manufacturers had _____ in Detroit. Millions of cars every year were made there.

advantage	carriage	engine	ordinary	tough

11. It was a difficult competition, but our team was _____ and made it to the end.

12. It is a great _____ to know the language of a country that you are visiting.

13. We took a ride around the park in an old _____ pulled by a white horse.

14. This was no _____ day. It was the day he got the job he had always dreamed of having.

15. His car doesn't work right now. There is something wrong with the _____ . He needs to have it repaired.

WORD FAMILIES

Fill in the blanks with words from each box.

demand *(noun)*	demand *(verb)*	demanding *(adjective)*

1. My classes are very _____ this semester. I have to study a lot.

2. The workers _____ to have better wages and working conditions.

| prosperity *(noun)* | prosper *(verb)* | prosperous *(adjective)* |

3. Detroit was very _____ in the early days of the auto industry. Then it had some economic problems.

4. Some experts say that India's economy will continue to grow and _____ because of computers.

| attachment *(noun)* | attach *(verb)* | attached *(adjective)* |

5. I sent him a file by e-mail. I sent the file as an _____ to the message.

6. His car is old, but he won't sell it. He's very _____ to it. He treats it like a favorite pet!

WRAP IT UP

DISCUSS THE THEME

Read these questions. Discuss your answers with a partner.

1. What is your favorite car? What does it look like? Is it a new car or an older car?

2. If you could have your own robot, what would you want it to do for you? Why?

3. What are the main industries of a town you know well? What would happen to the town if one or more of the industries left the town?

RESPOND IN WRITING

Look back at the unit and choose the passage you enjoyed the most. Read it again. Write a one-paragraph summary of the passage in your notebook.

What do you think is the most interesting thing about this passage, and why? Write a paragraph in your notebook.

CANADIAN HISTORY
THE YUKON

The Yukon

BEFORE YOU READ

Answer these questions.

1. In your opinion, what makes life exciting?

2. If you had the chance to do something adventurous, what would it be?

3. What are some things in life you consider valuable?

CHAPTER 1

Jack London, 1876–1916

PREPARE TO READ

Discuss these questions.

1. Do you like to read in your spare time? If yes, what kinds of books do you like to read?

2. Who is your favorite author?

WORD FOCUS

Match the words with their definitions.

A.

1. abandon ___   **a.** on purpose
2. deliberately ___   **b.** a person or thing that is not included
3. determination ___ **c.** the firm decision to succeed
4. devastate ___   **d.** leave someone or something forever
5. exception ___   **e.** destroy completely

B.

1. harsh ___   **a.** secret, very interesting plans
2. intrigue ___   **b.** a search for something
3. prolific ___   **c.** a great task
4. pursuit ___   **d.** producing a lot
5. undertaking ___ **e.** unpleasant; difficult

SCAN

Guess if this is true or false. Circle *a* or *b*.

Jack London lived an exciting life.

a. True   **b.** False

Scan the passage quickly to check your answer.

Jack London: Incredible Author, Incredible Life

Many people want a long, peaceful life. It is uncommon for someone to prefer a short but adventurous life. Jack London, one of the most brilliant authors of his time, was one such **exception**. His life was short, yet full of adventure, excitement, and **intrigue**. Jack London preferred it that way.

5 Jack London was born in San Francisco, California, on January 12, 1876. His real father **abandoned** his mother before Jack was born. When Jack was a baby, his mother married John London. Jack grew up with his mother and stepfather in a home where there was little money. As a teenager, Jack had to go to work in a factory to help with expenses
10 at home. In those days, there weren't strict laws yet against child labor. Jack worked all day without a break. At times, he even worked for two days straight. Jack was a hard worker, but the money he made was never enough. So, he thought of a way to earn more without having to work so hard.

15 Jack borrowed money from his aunt and bought a small boat. Jack became an oyster pirate, in other words, an oyster thief. Oysters are grown in special beds in the ocean and were a very popular type of seafood at that time. People bought oysters from pirates because the pirates sold the illegally collected oysters at a much lower price. Jack made far more money
20 from his illegal oyster business than in the factory. At 14, Jack worried about going to jail, so he stopped stealing oysters. He also quit school. Over the next few years, he worked at many different jobs. He went to Japan as a sailor, and he rode trains around the United States as a hobo, a homeless man.

25 Although Jack London was a good student and loved to read books, he only had gone to school through the 8th grade. Because of his **determination** and intelligence, Jack was later able to complete all of high school in one year. At age 19, he was admitted to the University of California at Berkeley. It seemed like an exciting new beginning. Yet the
30 excitement didn't last long. Jack had experienced the **harsh** realities of life from a very young age. Working hard to make a living, he had learned a lot about the world through personal experience. He felt that college offered a different type of education, but the reality was something different. Jack felt that this type of formal education lacked something. He only stayed at
35 Berkeley for six months. Bored with college and thirsty for more adventure, Jack decided to seek his fortune in Canada.

In the late 19th century, gold was discovered in the remote Klondike region of Canada's Yukon Territory, near Alaska. Thousands of men went to that distant land in hopes of finding gold. They were called prospectors.
40 Tempted by the idea of becoming rich, Jack went to Canada to become a gold prospector. Unfortunately, the harsh winter and difficult living conditions made it impossible for Jack to adjust. In addition, he became seriously ill because of the lack of fresh fruit and vegetables in his diet. Eventually, Jack returned home without any gold but full of exciting
45 new stories to tell. All of his experiences of adventure and intrigue in the Klondike and on the trip there led him to write his first stories.

continued

At first, Jack found it difficult to sell any of his stories. The first story he was able to sell was entitled "To the Man on Trail." This story was inspired by his days as a gold prospector in the Klondike. After that, Jack London was on his way to becoming the highest-paid and most-admired author of his time. He became a **prolific** writer. He wrote countless short stories and novels. He wrote 50 novels in 17 years, and he earned a lot of money. One reason he wrote so many novels was that he always spent more than he earned. He often found himself writing a novel in order to pay his bills. Some of his most famous books are *The Sea-Wolf, Call of the Wild,* and *The People of the Abyss.* It wasn't only his innate ability to write great stories that made him so successful. It was also his determination and hard work.

Jack London is thought by many to be one of the best writers of the 20th century. His restless spirit and never-ending **pursuit** of excitement led him to travel widely. As a result, he had a vast number of stories to share with the world. His adventurous, eventful life inspired him to write stories that captured the imagination of readers around the world.

His personal life was as intriguing as his written work. Jack was married twice. He had two daughters with his first wife. The love of his life was Charmian Kittredge, his secretary, who later became his second wife. With Charmian, he shared a life of adventure. They traveled extensively and even built a boat to sail together around the world. However, Jack developed health problems on the trip. They were only able to reach Australia before they had to return home.

Always in search of a new challenge, Jack decided to build the house of his dreams. This was an enormous **undertaking** that would end up costing him close to $80,000—a huge amount of money at that time. As soon as the house was ready and Jack and his wife were about to move in, a fire that some say was **deliberately** set, completely destroyed the house. This **devastated** Jack, but he didn't give up. He was determined to rebuild his dream house. Yet, he never did. A variety of health problems led Jack London to his early death on November 22, 1916.

At 40, Jack London had lived a short, but eventful life. He once said, "The proper function of man is to live, not to exist. I shall not waste my days in trying to prolong them. I shall use my time." Jack London used his time to its fullest. His enthusiasm, love for adventure, and excitement live on through the characters in his remarkable stories.

Read the passage again and answer the questions. Circle your answers.

MAIN IDEA

1. What is the main topic of the passage?
   A. Jack London's trip around the world
   B. the story of a famous author
   C. Jack London's most popular novels
   D. the exciting lives of two authors

DETAIL

2. Who lent Jack London the money for his boat?
   A. his mother
   B. his stepfather
   C. his aunt
   D. no one; he earned it himself

3. What did oyster pirates do?
   A. They bought oysters at a very high price.
   B. They stole oysters and sold them at a low price.
   C. They worked with the police to stop pirates.
   D. They sold oysters to pirates at a high price.

4. What is true about Jack London?
   A. He never finished high school.
   B. He attended college for a short time.
   C. He graduated from high school at age 14.
   D. He dropped out of school at age 8.

5. What jobs did Jack London have?
   A. sailor
   B. factory worker
   C. author
   D. all of the above

6. Why did Jack London leave Berkeley?
   A. He was bored.
   B. His mother was ill.
   C. He didn't have enough money.
   D. He had finished his degree.

7. What did Jack London do in the Klondike?
   A. He hunted for bears.
   B. He prospected for gold.
   C. He grew fruits and vegetables.
   D. He ran a large hotel.

8. What was the inspiration for his first published story?
   A. his life with his mother and stepfather
   B. his adventures as a prospector
   C. his time at Berkeley
   D. the love of his life

INFERENCE

9. Jack London might have written
   A. a story about a man lost in the snow
   B. a book about farming
   C. a history of France
   D. a biography of William Shakespeare

10. Jack London lived an eventful life because
    A. his life was short
    B. his life was full of adventure
    C. he didn't finish college
    D. he worked long hours in a factory

CHAPTER 2

Yukon, Canada welcome sign

PREPARE TO READ

Discuss these questions.

1. In your opinion, what is the most beautiful place on earth?

2. What is your favorite activity when you are on vacation?

WORD FOCUS

Match the words with their definitions.

A.
1. element ___
2. evident ___
3. habitat ___
4. melt ___
5. province ___

a. change from ice to water
b. one of the main divisions in some countries, similar to a state
c. one important part of something
d. the natural home of a plant or animal
e. clear; obvious

B.
1. reenergize ___
2. relax ___
3. species ___
4. spectacular ___
5. trace ___

a. spend time not doing much
b. give someone energy again
c. very beautiful or amazing
d. follow the development of something
e. a group of animals that are the same type

SCAN

Guess if this is true or false. Circle _a_ or _b_.

Yukon has a large population.

a. True   **b.** False

Scan the passage quickly to check your answer.

Yukon, Canada: A Place Beyond Time

We live in a world of incredible technological advancements, advancements that no one dreamed of even 50 years ago. Today, we are constantly connected to work, friends, family, and the world in general. We are able to fit more and more into our workdays, and work follows us
5 wherever we go. We have succeeded in making our daily lives easier and more connected with the help of science and technology. However, this comes with a price. People are experiencing higher levels of stress. We all need to find ways to reduce this stress. Everyone needs to find time to **relax**, at least once in a while.

10 There is a wild and remote place that can **reenergize** the body and spirit. This place allows visitors to exchange the modern world for nature, the hurried pace of city life for the calm of the wilderness. This place calls visitors away from those connections with the rest of the world, at least for a time. This place is Yukon, Canada.

15 ## Yukon Territory

The Yukon Territory is located in northwestern Canada, on the border with Alaska. This **province** is rich in history, but above all, it is rich in beauty. It is often called simply "the Yukon." This vast land covers 290,070 square miles (483,450 square kilometers). However, it has a population of just
20 30,000. The Yukon's landscape is truly **spectacular**. The breathtaking world of the Yukon includes steep mountains, lush green valleys, and undisturbed wildlife. It also includes a rich history dating back many thousands of years when native tribes first settled in the region. Canada's highest mountains are found in the Yukon. These include Mount Logan,
25 the second highest peak on the North American continent. Mount Logan is situated in Kluane National Park (pronounced *klu-wa-nee*), which is in the southwestern part of Yukon.

Kluane National Park is one of Canada's most precious gems. Snowcapped mountains tower over long, deep valleys. Immense glaciers
30 top mountains and extend across valleys and wide sections of land. These vast fields of snow and ice have existed for thousands of years. The glaciers **melt** slowly in the summer months, and the winter adds deep new layers of snow. Water from the glaciers and melting snow finds its way into the rushing streams and rivers.

35 Kluane is the home of an incredible variety of wildlife. Visitors can spot huge grizzly bears roaming about in search of berries or catching salmon in the rivers. Mountain goats, black bears, wolves, and caribou are some of the larger animals in Kluane National Park. Countless smaller creatures include foxes, rabbits, and beavers. This is also the **habitat** for
40 over 150 **species** of birds. Several of the animals in the Yukon have coats that change to white in winter. This lets them blend in with the snow that covers the land. It helps them hide from their enemies.

Besides the breathtaking landscapes and diverse wildlife, Kluane National Park is the homeland of the Southern Tutchone tribe. These
45 Native Canadians **trace** their culture back in history thousands of years.

continued

They have made their living hunting and fishing. An important **element** of this culture has been a deep love and respect for nature and wildlife. The Tutchone only hunt animals for survival, not for pleasure. Their love of nature is **evident** in the fascinating stories passed on from one generation
50 to the next. One such story is about the fox and the bear. Legend has it that the bear got jealous of the fox's long tail. When the bear asked the fox why its tail was so long, the fox replied, "That way I can catch fish more easily." The fox showed the bear how easy it was to catch fish by sticking its tail in the ice. When the bear tried to do the same, its tail froze. According
55 to the legend, that is the reason all bears have short tails.

The Klondike Gold Rush

The Tutchone people are responsible for an important discovery. They were the first to find gold in the region in the late 1800s. This led to the Klondike Gold Rush. Skookum Jim and Tagish Charlie first discovered a
60 nugget, or piece, of gold next to the Klondike River. After the news spread throughout the Yukon and around the world, a rush of gold prospectors flooded the area. This is when the famous city of Dawson was founded. During the Gold Rush, Dawson was one of the busiest cities in the world. Thousands of people settled in the area in hopes of finding gold. Most
65 eventually left, and today, Dawson is mainly a tourist attraction. Visitors can visit the Klondike River and pan for gold, remove gold from the water, just like prospectors did a hundred years ago.

There are endless natural wonders to see and equally exciting things to do in the Yukon. Visitors can take supervised wilderness tours, sign up
70 for kayaking and river-rafting, go camping, hiking, fishing, and horse-back riding. Visitors can even participate in a mountain bike race. Yukon is one of the top areas in the world for mountain biking. Every year, approximately 7,000 cyclists participate in this exciting race.

Travel agencies offer guided trips that combine a range of different
75 activities. This is a fun and exciting way to discover the beauty of the Yukon. For example, on the first day of the trip, visitors can paddle down the Yukon River and camp overnight next to the river. On the second day, visitors can take a ride on a riverboat and observe the diverse wildlife. Next, hiking takes them through lush valleys and over scenic trails. The trip
80 can't be complete without visiting the legendary Dawson City, where there is still a good chance of finding gold.

Any way you decide to explore this incredible place, one thing is certain. All the worries and stress of everyday life will disappear somewhere in the Yukon. It is truly an opportunity of a lifetime to travel through this
85 spectacular place and take in all the wonders that nature has to offer.

Read the passage again and answer the questions. Circle your answers.

MAIN IDEA

1. What is the main topic of the passage?
   - **A.** an incredible place in Canada
   - **B.** a modern city
   - **C.** Kluane National Park
   - **D.** Canada

DETAIL

2. Why do people need relaxation?
   - **A.** to reduce stress
   - **B.** to be connected to work and friends
   - **C.** to appreciate better science and technology
   - **D.** to increase stress

3. Yukon's population is about
   - **A.** 3,000
   - **B.** 30,000
   - **C.** 300,000
   - **D.** 3,000,000

4. What is the second highest mountain peak in North America called?
   - **A.** Yukon
   - **B.** Kluane
   - **C.** Southern Tutchone
   - **D.** Mount Logan

5. What are some examples of wildlife mentioned in the passage?
   - **A.** grizzly and black bears
   - **B.** mountain goats and birds
   - **C.** wolves and caribou
   - **D.** all of the above

6. What is an important contribution of the Tutchone people?
   - **A.** their discovery of gold
   - **B.** their beautiful jewelry
   - **C.** the city of Dawson
   - **D.** all of the above

7. According to the legend, what happened to the bear?
   - **A.** The bear's tail froze while fishing.
   - **B.** The bear got angry at an eagle.
   - **C.** The bear's tail grew longer.
   - **D.** The bear fell into the river.

8. What activities are mentioned in the passage?
   - **A.** roller-skating and swimming
   - **B.** swimming and golfing
   - **C.** kayaking and river-rafting
   - **D.** hiking and snowboarding

INFERENCE

9. Why is the Yukon an exciting place to visit?
   - **A.** because it is the largest city in Canada
   - **B.** because people can experience higher levels of stress
   - **C.** because there are many things to see and do
   - **D.** because the people are friendly

10. What makes the city of Dawson a legendary place?
    - **A.** its history
    - **B.** its restaurants
    - **C.** its travel agencies
    - **D.** its visitors

CHAPTER 3

◀ Panning for gold

PREPARE TO READ

Discuss these questions.

1. What is the most precious metal or gem in your culture?

2. Can you think of some ways people around the world have used gold?

WORD FOCUS

Match the words with their definitions.

A.
1. artifact ____   **a.** a long rubber or plastic tube
2. elaborate ____   **b.** a scientist who studies rocks
3. excavation ____   **c.** very complicated
4. geologist ____   **d.** digging for something in the ground
5. hose ____   **e.** an object of cultural interest made by a person

B.
1. origin ____   **a.** an official paper that says you are allowed to do something
2. permit ____   **b.** a long line of a mineral such as gold inside another solid rock
3. process ____   **c.** worth the cost or effort
4. vein ____   **d.** the place where something started
5. worthwhile ____   **e.** a series of steps for a particular purpose

SCAN

Guess if this is true or false. Circle *a* or *b*.

Pyrite is called "fool's gold."

a. True   **b.** False

Scan the passage quickly to check your answer.

Gold: The Precious Metal

Homer, the Greek poet of ancient times, called it "the glory of the gods." The Incas called it "the tears of the sun." Homer described its enormous value to humans, while the Incas captured its incredible natural beauty. Gold is indeed the most precious and beautiful metal of all times. It is also the most sought-after and most traded metal in history.

The History of Gold

Gold has always been greatly valued. Ancient civilizations like the Phoenicians, the Greeks, the Egyptians, the Chinese, and so many others used gold to make **artifacts** and even items of worship. **Excavations** have unearthed gold vases, cups, plates, and, of course, jewelry. Around 700 b.c., Lydian merchants and traders made the first gold coins. The Greeks used gold for their official money. Gold is universally accepted as backing for the world's currencies.

Mining Methods

The Greeks mined gold all around the Mediterranean region. Their mining method was simple, yet very creative. They used water and a sheep's fleece, or skin, to separate the gold from the dirt. The fleece would absorb the mixture of water, sand, and gold. All they had to do was let the fleece dry out and then shake it gently to collect the flakes of gold.

Underground gold mines were common in the past. Lone prospectors searched rock formations for signs of a gold **vein**. Often this was in desert areas where soil did not cover the rocks. Once a vein of gold was discovered in a rock formation, a mine was built into the hillside. Many stories from the Old West tell of prospectors digging unsuccessfully for gold their entire lives. The dusty old prospector with his donkey and shovels appears in many movies. Still other legends exist about lost mines containing fabulous gold deposits. Even today, people search for these lost mines.

Another method for mining gold is panning. This method was widely used during the Gold Rush in the 1800s. Prospectors worked in a shallow part of a river. They used a pan filled with water to separate gold from the small rocks and dirt. However, panning was a very slow **process**. When they were lucky, the prospectors found small flakes of gold. Some lucky men found a small nugget. Most of the time, they found nothing but dirt. Eventually, this method was abandoned for other methods that produced better results.

One method that produced more gold faster is the hydraulic method. The hydraulic method uses the power of water. This method finds its **origin** in Ancient Greece. Remember how the Greeks used the fleece and water to collect gold? That was a primitive form of the hydraulic method. In modern times, this method developed into a more **elaborate**, but destructive technique. Water was directed onto a hillside through a **hose** at high pressure. The jet of water struck the hillside with great force. The force tore the hill apart, exposing the gold. This technique had a significant impact on the environment. All the dirt that was left was dumped into the

continued

nearest stream. This polluted the water and destroyed wildlife. It was time for a safer method.

Now, gold mining employs, or uses, technology. First, **geologists** explore an area where they believe gold may be found. After they identify a possible location, drilling begins. Drilling equipment brings rock to the surface. The rock is tested for gold. In the next stage, mining engineers determine whether it is **worthwhile** to mine the area. The engineers may find that the soil won't allow for safe mining, or that there isn't enough gold, or that the wildlife in this particular location may be in danger if they proceed with the mining operations. After all the initial testing is complete, the construction of the mine can begin.

The building of a new surface mine in Canada or the United States is a very complicated process. Support facilities need to be built for the engineers and workers. Depending on the size and location of the project, an entire town may need to be developed. Of course, all construction must have approval and the necessary **permits** from local government agencies. Mining can cause a lot of damage to the environment, so the mining company must follow strict environmental laws. For example, water quality must be protected. There also must be a formal plan to reclaim the area after the mining project is completed. Reclaiming means restoring the land back to its original state. A reclamation project usually includes planting trees. Thus, the mining company must budget for restoration of the land after the completion of the project.

Although gold mining technology has advanced, there are still many serious environmental issues. One major concern involves the use of a very toxic chemical to separate gold from other materials. This chemical is called cyanide. This highly toxic chemical can kill humans and wildlife. In Canada and the United States, mining companies must ensure that cyanide is not dumped into the environment. It must be retrieved and recycled properly. Recent technology uses special treatments to reduce the harmful effects of cyanide.

Mining for Tourists

There is still fascination with the older methods of gold mining. Nowadays, certain tourist sites offer panning for recreation purposes. People can get a taste of what it felt like to be a gold prospector. One place that offers visitors the opportunity to experience gold panning is Sutter Gold Mine in Sutter Creek, California. An actual mine back in the 1880s, Sutter Gold Mine is now open only for entertainment purposes. Visitors can experience gold panning for a small fee. In addition, one-hour tours of the mine educate guests on the different mining methods and equipment used. Visitors can also learn how to differentiate between real gold deposits and pyrite, a yellow deposit of minerals that is often mistaken for gold. Pyrite is actually known as "fool's gold."

Gold mining continues to be as important today as it was thousands of years ago. The desire for gold has not diminished over time nor has the excitement of discovery. Gold is still truly "the glory of the gods."

Read the passage again and answer the questions. Circle your answers.

MAIN IDEA

1. What is the main topic of the passage?
   A. the golden fleece
   B. gold artifacts
   C. mining gold
   D. famous gold mines

DETAIL

2. Why is gold considered "the precious metal"?
   A. because it is shiny
   B. because it was used to make artifacts
   C. because it is the most sought-after and traded
   D. because it was used as money

3. What gold items did ancient civilizations use?
   A. jewelry
   B. vases, cups, and plates
   C. items of worship
   D. all of the above

4. Who made the first gold coins?
   A. Lydian merchants
   B. Greek merchants
   C. Egyptian traders
   D. Chinese traders

5. What signs of gold did prospectors look for?
   A. rock formations
   B. special trees
   C. abandoned mines
   D. sheep

6. What is panning?
   A. the excavation of ancient artifacts
   B. a method for mining gold
   C. using a sheep's fleece to collect gold
   D. a modern method

7. What is the first step in modern gold mining?
   A. Geologists explore the area.
   B. Workers excavate the area.
   C. Workers begin drilling.
   D. Mining engineers construct the mine.

8. What can we say about panning today?
   A. It is the best way to mine gold.
   B. It produces dangerous chemicals.
   C. It is used for recreation purposes.
   D. No one pans for gold anymore.

INFERENCE

9. What can you infer about modern gold mining?
   A. It is a very simple process.
   B. It always requires an entire town to be developed.
   C. It can be harmful to the environment.
   D. all of the above

10. Which of the following is probably true?
    A. Gold is no longer a popular metal for jewelry.
    B. People continue to be fascinated by gold.
    C. Mining techniques have changed little over time.
    D. Most people have no desire to own gold.

VOCABULARY REVIEW

WHICH MEANING?

From Chapter 1: *Jack London: Incredible Author, Incredible Life*

1. What does *straight* mean in the following sentence?

    > At times, he even worked for two days straight.

    A. straight *(adverb)* in an honest and direct way
    B. straight *(adverb)* without stopping
    C. straight *(adjective)* in a line

From Chapter 2: *Yukon, Canada: A Place Beyond Time*

2. What does *spot* mean in the following sentence?

    > Visitors can spot huge grizzly bears roaming about in search of berries or catching salmon in the rivers.

    A. spot *(noun)* a particular place or area
    B. spot *(noun)* a small round mark
    C. spot *(verb)* to see

From Chapter 3: *Gold: The Precious Metal*

3. What does *deposit* mean in the following sentence?

    > Still other legends exist about lost mines containing fabulous gold deposits.

    A. deposit *(noun)* an amount of money put into a bank
    B. deposit *(noun)* an amount of money that is the first payment for something
    C. deposit *(noun)* something in the ground that is the result of a natural process

WRONG WORD

One word in each group does not fit. Circle the word.

1. harsh	pursuit	problems	difficult
2. plentiful	prolific	productive	province
3. relax	old	elderly	ancient
4. evident	clear	obvious	process
5. devastate	worthwhile	valuable	useful
6. artifacts	dig	intrigue	excavation

WORDS IN CONTEXT

Fill in the blanks with words from each box.

elaborate	element	pursuit	relax	species

1. The _____ of happiness is a characteristic of all people.

2. Many people visit spas to _____.

3. We saw several different _____ of birds in the park.

4. The main _____ of a great novel is a great story.

5. The company presented its _____ plan to remove the gold from the rock.

artifacts	devastated	provinces	trace	worthwhile

6. Spending so many hours studying is _____. One day, it will pay off.

7. Gold _____ from the site included cups, vases, and jewelry.

8. Yukon Territory is one of the Canadian _____. It covers many thousands of square miles.

9. A huge hurricane _____ the city of New Orleans.

10. They can _____ their family line back 400 years.

exceptions	geologists	permit	spectacular	undertaking

11. You need to make sure you have a building _____ before you start to build a house.

12. The view from the top of the mountain was _____.

13. Building a new mine is a major _____. A lot of work must be done before gold is produced.

14. The company hired a team of _____ to search for oil.

15. There are no _____ to the rule. Everyone must have a driver's license.

WORD FAMILIES

Fill in the blanks with words from each box.

deliberation *(noun)*	deliberate *(adjective)*	deliberately *(adverb)*

1. She made a _____ attempt to stop the man from leaving.

2. You _____ threw that book on the floor! Why didn't you put it on the table?

| contribution *(noun)* | contribute *(verb)* | contributing *(adjective)* |

3. His constant complaining was a _____ factor to his getting fired.

4. An anonymous donor made a million-dollar _____ to the Red Cross.

| elaboration *(noun)* | elaborate *(verb)* | elaborate *(adjective)* |

5. The director asked his employee to _____ on her idea so everyone could understand it better.

6. They designed an _____ plan to rob the bank in three minutes.

WRAP IT UP

DISCUSS THE THEME

Read these questions and discuss them with your partner.

1. Which adventure would you find more exciting: searching for gold, exploring the wilderness, or sailing around the world? Why?

2. People to this day are fascinated with gold. Do you like gold? How do people in your culture feel about gold?

3. How do you measure success? Discuss whether you think wealthy living is successful living.

RESPOND IN WRITING

Look back at the unit and choose the passage you enjoyed the most. Read it again. Write a one-paragraph summary of the passage in your notebook.

What do you think is the most interesting thing about this passage, and why? Write a paragraph in your notebook.

TECHNOLOGY
COMMUNICATIONS

Satellite dishes in Socorro, New Mexico

BEFORE YOU READ

Answer these questions.

1. Who are some of the great inventors in history? What did they invent?

2. What technology do you use most often?

3. How have cell phones changed our lives?

CHAPTER 1

Alexander Graham
Bell, 1847–1922

Bell's telephone

PREPARE TO READ

Discuss these questions.

1. What do you know about Alexander Graham Bell?

2. Have you ever had an idea for an invention? If so, what?

WORD FOCUS

Match the words with their definitions.

A.
1. challenge ____
2. commonplace ____
3. controversial ____
4. exchange ____
5. fiber optics ____

a. giving or receiving something in return for something else
b. the use of thin fibers of glass to send signals
c. not very exciting or unusual; ordinary
d. invite someone to do something that is difficult
e. causing much disagreement

B.
1. patent ____
2. telecommunication ____
3. translation ____
4. transmit ____
5. vocal chords ____

a. changing something from one language to another
b. thin muscles in the throat that move to produce sound
c. send out electronic signals
d. communication at a distance using electronic equipment
e. an official license that gives one person rights and prevents others from copying a product

SCAN

Guess if this is true or false. Circle *a* or *b*.

Alexander Graham Bell developed a speaking machine with his brother.

a. True   **b.** False

Scan the passage quickly to check your answer.

Alexander Graham Bell: Father of the Telephone

Alexander Graham Bell's discoveries help us connect with people all over the world. His inventions in the 19th century led to much of the **telecommunications** technology in use today.

Bell was born on March 3, 1847 in Edinburgh, Scotland. His birth
5 name was Alexander Bell. He added the name Graham in 1858 to honor a family friend. Even as a child, communications interested him. This was logical given his family's interests. His grandfather, father, and uncle all taught speech. All of the Bell men had wonderful speaking voices.

Bell's mother Eliza Grace Symonds Bell was deaf. Even though she
10 couldn't hear, she was an excellent pianist. As a boy, Alexander was very aware of how sounds were made. Alexander spoke to his mother in a low tone with his mouth very close to her forehead. Everyone else talked to his mother through a special ear tube. He understood that she could feel the sounds.

15 At the age of 13, Alexander Bell finished high school. When he was 14, he visited London with his father. There, Bell saw a "speaking machine" that Sir Charles Wheatstone had made. On his return home, his father **challenged** Alexander and his older brother to invent their own "speaking machine." They created a machine that made human-like sounds.

20 Bell used his dog to study how sounds are made. He practiced moving his dog's mouth and **vocal chords**. He was able to make the dog's barks sound like words.

In 1864, Bell began studying at the University of Edinburgh. He continued his studies at the University of London in 1868. While he was
25 studying at the university, Bell also taught. Bell studied the writings of a German scientist named Von Helmholtz. Von Helmholtz was working with telegraphs and sound transmission. Bell couldn't read German, and he made a famous mistake in his **translations**. He mistakenly thought that Von Helmholtz said that vowel sounds could be **transmitted** over a
30 wire. This mistake would be very important to Bell's development of the telephone. It caused him to consider a new possibility. In just a few years, the idea that people could talk over a wire would become **commonplace**.

By 1870, Bell's two brothers had died. Bell moved to Canada with his parents. In Canada, he began working on different communication
35 machines. One such machine was a piano that sent sounds over a distance using electricity.

The following year, Bell moved to Boston. He taught deaf students at several schools in the Boston area, and he had private students as well. Bell taught the deaf to read lips and to speak. Many people didn't like his way
40 of teaching. They thought that teaching sign language was the only way to teach deaf students to communicate.

In 1873, Bell began teaching at Boston University. There, he met Mabel Hubbard, his future wife. Mabel, who was one of his private students, was deaf. They married in 1877. They had two daughters, Elsie May and
45 Marian, and two sons, Edward and Robert, but both boys died at birth.

continued

The idea for the telephone occurred to Bell while he was visiting his parents in Canada during the summer of 1874. Back in Boston, Bell met Thomas Watson. Watson, who worked as a mechanic and model maker, sometimes helped inventors. Soon Watson was working with Bell regularly
50 as his assistant.

On February 14, 1876, Bell filed a **patent** application with the United States Patent Office for his telephone. A patent gives a person legal rights to any money earned from an invention. It also proves that the person who filed the patent was the first to invent the device. Less than a month later,
55 on March 7, 1876, a patent was issued for Bell's telephone. On March 10, 1876, the first human voice was heard over the telephone. This brief **exchange** took place between Bell and Watson at Bell's home in Boston. The story is that Bell spilled acid from a battery onto his clothing. He reportedly said, "Mr. Watson, come here. I want you." The exact nature of
60 the exchange is uncertain. What is clear is that a voice transmission took place.

The telephone very quickly became important to the world. Bell first presented his telephone to the public in Philadelphia in 1876. By 1878, a telephone was installed in the White House. The first call, of course, was to
65 Alexander Graham Bell.

The invention of the telephone was **controversial** because other people claimed to have invented it, too. Over the course of his life, Bell fought 600 lawsuits and won each one.

After the telephone, Bell worked on many other projects. Many of his
70 ideas are only now coming into use. One of these was a system to send sounds on a beam of light. The machine was called a photophone. That research became important in the development of **fiber optics**, which are used today to transmit light, images, and sound. Bell also invented a metal detector, an airplane, and a hydrofoil—a machine that "flies" on the water.
75 In all, Bell held 30 patents. By the age of 30, Bell was very rich.

This great inventor knew many famous people of his time. In 1887, he met Helen Keller. She had lost both her hearing and her sight as a very young girl. Bell helped her family find a teacher for her, Anne Sullivan. The relationship between Helen Keller and Anne Sullivan is a famous story of
80 triumph over hardship.

Throughout his life Bell also worked to promote the love of science and education, and he earned many honors. In 1882, he became a citizen of the United States. He was one of the founding members of the National Geographic Society in 1888.

85 Alexander Graham Bell died on August 2, 1922. He was buried at his summer home in Nova Scotia in Canada. On that day, all telephones stopped ringing for one minute to honor the man who made such important contributions to the field of communications.

Read the passage again and answer the questions. Circle your answers.

MAIN IDEA

1. What is the main topic of the passage?
   A. the invention of the telephone
   B. the life of Alexander Graham Bell
   C. the teaching of deaf people
   D. the invention of the photophone

DETAIL

2. Where was Alexander Graham Bell born?
   A. Boston
   B. Nova Scotia
   C. Edinburgh
   D. Philadelphia

3. What did Bell's father challenge him to do?
   A. teach his dog to talk
   B. build a speaking machine
   C. teach his mother to talk
   D. invent sign language

4. What job did Bell have when he moved to Boston?
   A. He taught deaf students.
   B. He was a full-time inventor.
   C. He taught speech.
   D. He worked as an electrician.

5. What did Bell's mother and wife have in common?
   A. They were both born in Scotland.
   B. They were both named Eliza.
   C. They were both deaf.
   D. They both died in childbirth.

6. How many lawsuits did Bell fight and win during his life?
   A. 200
   B. 400
   C. 600
   D. 800

7. Which of the following statements is true?
   A. Bell's inventions did not earn much, and he died a poor man.
   B. Bell's inventions made him rich at a young age.
   C. Bell's inventions have been of little use in recent years.
   D. Bell sold his patents to the U.S. government.

8. Which of the following is **not** one of Bell's ideas?
   A. telephone
   B. record player
   C. hydrofoil
   D. metal detector

INFERENCE

9. Which of the following was one of Bell's main interests?
   A. helping deaf people speak
   B. selling telephones to everyone
   C. earning as much money as he could
   D. filing lawsuits

10. What can we say about Bell?
    A. He tried unsuccessfully to build a record player.
    B. His only invention was the telephone.
    C. He was interested only in inventing things.
    D. His invention was one of the most important in history.

CHAPTER 2

Statue of Paul Revere in Boston, Massachusetts

PREPARE TO READ

Discuss these questions.

1. What do you know about the history of Boston?

2. What do you know about modern-day Boston?

WORD FOCUS

Match the words with their definitions.

A.

1. fireworks ___   **a.** noisy, colorful explosives used for entertainment
2. house ___   **b.** a running race that is 26 miles (42 km) long
3. incident ___   **c.** the state of being free
4. independence ___   **d.** contain or keep something
5. marathon ___   **e.** an event that involves something dangerous or strange

B.

1. newsletter ___   **a.** a person who plays a sport for money
2. patriot ___   **b.** a printed report similar to a newspaper
3. professional ___   **c.** a place where people live for the first time
4. settlement ___   **d.** cloth that is made to use in clothing
5. textile ___   **e.** a person who loves his/her country

SCAN

Guess if this is true or false. Circle *a* or *b*.

The first public library in the United States was in Boston.

a. True   **b.** False

Scan the passage quickly to check your answer.

Boston: A City of Firsts

Boston, Massachusetts is a city of firsts. It was one of the first European **settlements** in the "New World." It was the first city to turn against the British government. It **houses** the oldest university in America. It was and is home to many inventors. Alexander Graham Bell made his famous
5 first telephone call in Boston. The light bulb, the instant camera, and the portable razor were all invented in Boston.

The first English immigrant to arrive in Boston was William Blackstone. He came in 1629 to a place called Shawmut. This was the name given to the area by local Native Americans. The next year, Blackstone's friend John
10 Winthrop arrived with his group of English Puritans. They first settled north of Salem. They didn't like the area, so Blackstone suggested that they settle in Shawmut. Winthrop renamed the village Boston. For the next 200 years, Boston was the center of Puritan life.

Other things happened in Boston first. The first school in the British
15 colony was started there in 1635, the Boston Latin School. This public school is still in operation. The following year Harvard, the nation's oldest college, was founded.

Because of its location on a harbor, Boston was the leading center of business and trade for the American colonies. It was a great shipbuilding
20 center for the world. It was also the primary port in North America for sending and receiving goods.

Boston was important because of its role in America's **independence**. By the mid-1700s, there were major problems between England and its American colonies. Many of the leaders of the fight for independence lived
25 in Boston, including John Quincy Adams and Benjamin Franklin. Many famous **incidents** that led up to the American Revolution took place in or near Boston. The Boston Tea Party and Paul Revere's famous ride are two of these. The battle that started the American Revolution took place just outside of Boston. Many **patriots** of the revolution have Boston as their
30 final resting place.

In the 19th century, Boston continued to grow. It was one of the world's richest cities. It was still a major trading port. It was famous for **textiles**, leather goods, and machinery. The city also continued as a leader in education.

35 Boston was again politically important in the years leading up to the U.S. Civil War that began in 1861. In 1831, William Lloyd Garrison had started *The Liberator*. This **newsletter** made Boston one of the first cities to call for the end of slavery. Many of the supplies needed for the Civil War came from Boston. Weapons, shoes, blankets, clothes, and other supplies
40 were made in the city.

During the 19th century, Boston was the center for industry and technology, much of it in communications. Samuel Morse, who invented the telegraph, was born in Boston. Boston was also home to Eli Whitney, the inventor of the cotton gin. This machine to remove seeds from cotton
45 changed life in the South. Thomas Edison was living in Boston when

continued

he worked on his light bulb. Alexander Graham Bell, the inventor of the telephone, lived in Boston at the time of his invention.

Interestingly, Bell and Edison both worked on ideas for telephone systems at the same time. In fact, Bell rented the same building that
50 Edison had rented. Lamar Latimer, an African American inventor, worked for both men. Latimer improved Edison's light bulb. He also helped Bell with his drawings of the telephone.

Several presidents have lived or studied in Boston. These include John Quincy Adams and John F. Kennedy. Boston was also a center for
55 literature, and it was home to the first public library. Many American writers are associated with Boston. Nathaniel Hawthorne, Ralph Waldo Emerson, Oliver Wendell Holmes, Henry David Thoreau, Edgar Allen Poe, Louisa May Alcott, and Henry James are just a few of the famous authors who lived in the city at one time.

60 Another first during the 19th century was the opening of the Boston subway system. It opened on September 1, 1897. It was the first underground transportation system in North America.

In the early 20th century, Boston suffered the same problems as the rest of the country. Many businesses closed because of the Great Depression
65 and the two world wars. Many people lost their jobs. By 1970, business had improved again, especially in finance and in technology. With over 100 universities in the area, many students who graduated stayed in Boston. They worked in and founded many technology and communication companies.

70 Almost 600,000 people live in Boston today. Because it is on a peninsula at the mouth of a river, there was never much room for the city to grow. To make more land, the city filled in the bay with soil. Almost half of the land in Boston was originally water. When people think of modern-day Boston, many things come to mind. Famous foods are clam chowder, lobster,
75 Boston cream pie, and baked beans. In fact, Boston is often called "Bean Town."

When it comes to music, Boston is famous for the Boston Philharmonic Orchestra and the Boston Pops. Every year on the Fourth of July, the Boston Pops plays along the Charles River and the city shares a spectacular
80 **fireworks** display with the whole country.

In the area of sports, Boston has many **professional** teams. The city has hockey, football, basketball, and baseball teams. The Boston Red Sox, the baseball team, won the very first World Series that was ever played in 1903. In the 2004 season, the Boston Red Sox won the World Series, and the
85 New England Patriots won the world championship in football. One of the most famous annual sporting events is the Boston **Marathon**. This race has been run every year for over 100 years. Runners from around the world come to Boston to compete.

Over the years, Boston has led the nation in many ways. In fact, Boston
90 is a city of leaders. Presidents, patriots, and inventors have called it home. Whether it is leading a nation to freedom, developing new communication technologies, or winning championships, Boston is a city of firsts.

Read the passage again and answer the questions. Circle your answers.

MAIN IDEA

1. What is the main topic of this passage?
   A. Boston's role in America's independence
   B. the many universities in Boston
   C. the many sports teams in Boston
   D. the history of Boston

DETAIL

2. Boston was founded by
   A. a group of Irish immigrants
   B. John Quincy Adams
   C. a group of Puritans
   D. Paul Revere

3. Because of its location, Boston has been very important for what?
   A. trade
   B. tourism
   C. politics
   D. education

4. What was *The Liberator*?
   A. a current Boston newspaper
   B. a newsletter
   C. a Revolutionary War paper
   D. a literary work by Nathaniel Hawthorne

5. Which of the following was invented in Boston?
   A. cotton cloth
   B. the telephone
   C. photographs
   D. the phonograph

6. Lamar Latimer helped which inventors?
   A. Alexander Graham Bell and Samuel Morse
   B. Thomas Edison and Alexander Graham Bell
   C. Eli Whitney and Thomas Edison
   D. Samuel Morse and Eli Whitney

7. In order to continue to grow, the city of Boston
   A. filled parts of the bay with dirt
   B. gave land to people
   C. built factories for businesses
   D. asked people to move to the city

8. Which of the following statements is true?
   A. Boston has a baseball team but not a football team.
   B. Boston has always had plenty of land for people to build on.
   C. Boston was of little importance in the years before the Civil War.
   D. Boston holds a marathon every year.

INFERENCE

9. What made Boston a good place to settle in the 1600s?
   A. its location on the coast
   B. its transportation system
   C. its help for inventors
   D. all of the above

10. Boston has been a leader in technology because
    A. it has so many universities
    B. it has the oldest subway system
    C. it was the home of patriots
    D. all of the above

CHAPTER 3

An early cell phone

PREPARE TO READ

Discuss these questions.

1. How many different ways can we send messages to other people?

2. How would you describe a cell phone to someone who has never used one?

WORD FOCUS

Match the words with their definitions.

A.
1. advance ___   **a.** something new
2. code ___   **b.** find the meaning of something that is in code
3. decode ___   **c.** a system of words, letters, or numbers instead of words
4. distance ___   **d.** a movement or progress forward
5. innovation ___   **e.** the space between two points

B.
1. limitation ___   **a.** make something as good as possible
2. option ___   **b.** a condition that makes something less useful
3. perfect ___   **c.** change something completely
4. revolutionize ___   **d.** connected with seeing
5. visual ___   **e.** a choice

SCAN

Guess if this is true or false. Circle *a* or *b*.

The first cell phone was made by Nikola Tesla.

a. True   **b.** False

Scan the passage quickly to check your answer.

Communicating with the World

People have always found ways to communicate with each other across **distances**. For most of history, communication could be only as fast as people, their horses, or their ships could travel. When our ancestors wanted to communicate over distance, they had few **options**.

5   In the past, people could send **visual** messages with fire and smoke. People could also use instruments such as drums or horns to send sounds. Sometimes people used pigeons, a type of bird, to send messages. Pigeons have an amazing ability to find their way home. Armies often took pigeons with them when they fought in wars. The soldiers attached small messages
10 to the pigeons and sent the birds flying home. Methods like these were used in many parts of the world for a long time. However, each of these ancient methods has serious **limitations**. Wind can blow smoke away, drum sounds can only travel a relatively short distance, and pigeons can only carry a small message.

15   People have always searched for ways to send messages as quickly and precisely as possible. Each new **advance** in communications opens up more possibilities, and so the search continues for something even better, faster, and more powerful.

    Many inventions in the last two centuries have helped people send
20 messages. In 1840, Samuel Morse developed the telegraph. The telegraph **revolutionized** communication. It allowed people to send messages instantly by transmitting electrical signals along a wire. The sender tapped in a **code**. The person at the other end of the wire would **decode** the signals. This person would then write the message in regular language.

25   There were some problems with the telegraph. The telegraph needed wire between different places. A trained person had to send or decode the message. Because of this, telegraph offices weren't common. Someone also had to deliver the message to the intended receiver. Also, until waterproof cable was developed, telegraphs could not be sent across the ocean to
30 Europe.

    The year 1876 brought one of the greatest inventions of all time: the telephone. This **innovation** in communication was invented by Alexander Graham Bell. However, Bell wasn't the only person working on a telephone system. Other inventors such as Antonio Miucci were trying to develop
35 a system of their own. Bell, however, still generally gets the credit for the invention of the telephone. The name Bell was for many years synonymous with the U.S. phone system. Bell was able to sell his version of the telephone, and he worked hard to make people aware of its possibilities. After he invented the telephone, Bell spent the next few years **perfecting**
40 his invention. He also traveled around the world, showing people how it worked.

    Although the telephone was amazing, it had problems. Like the telegraph, it required miles of wires to connect one phone to another. For many years, human operators also had to connect callers to each other.
45 In 1889, Almon Strowger developed a way to connect callers without a human operator. He invented a dialing system for telephones. To use his

continued

system, each telephone needed a unique number. Then people could make telephone calls without an operator.

Over the years, the telephone went through many changes. One
50 innovative worker tied the microphone and the earpiece together. He did this so that he could keep one hand free while using the telephone. This resulted in the receiver that we know today. Touch-tone dialing was a major improvement. This eventually allowed phones to work with computers.

Despite improvements, the need for wires was still a major limitation.
55 Inventors like Nikola Tesla and Guglielmo Marconi worked to find ways to send electronic signals without wires. These men learned that natural radio waves could carry sounds. With a transmitter and a receiver, these inventors figured out how to send sounds without wires.

By 1896, Marconi had developed the first wireless telegraph. The first
60 voice was sent over radio waves in 1906. The first song was heard on a radio in 1910. After years of controversy, Tesla was finally credited with the invention of the radio.

Wireless transmission allowed for many changes in the telephone. By 1927, the first radio telephone service operated between Britain and the
65 United States. The first mobile carphone came in 1946. In the late 1950s, this mobile system came into use in large cities for taxis and police. In 1965, the first home cordless telephone came out. This was a simple radio phone that used the base as the transmitter and the handset as the receiver.

The cellular telephone system started April 3, 1973. On that day, Dr.
70 Martin Cooper made the first call on a portable cellular phone. As he walked down the street in New York, people must have thought he looked odd: a man standing on the street talking on a phone without wires. Who would have imagined a day when so many people would be walking and talking at the same time?

75 Cell phones allow us to do so much more than just send and receive calls. We can send e-mails or instant text messages. We can access the Internet, watch television, listen to songs, take pictures or video, and play games with a phone as small as the palm of our hand.

Today's cell phones still aren't as reliable as landline telephones, but
80 improvements are on the way. New technology lets cell phones "talk" to other machines. Monitors, keyboards, and printers can "talk" to computers without the need for cables. Now cell phones, computers, personal digital assistants (PDAs), and even wired telephones can talk to each other. Right now, these devices must be no more than 30 feet (10 m) away from each
85 other to communicate. Before long, technology will be able to connect cell phones to computers at greater distances.

Someday we will be able to use our cell phones to start the car, turn on the oven to heat dinner, or turn on the lights when we get home. The cell phone of tomorrow could connect to literally any device with a computer
90 chip. Who knows what the future of telecommunications holds?

Read the passage again and answer the questions. Circle your answers.

MAIN IDEA

1. What is the main topic of this passage?
   A. the invention of the radio
   B. the invention of the telephone
   C. the invention of the telegraph
   D. innovations in communications

DETAIL

2. One problem with the telephone and telegraph was that
   A. they were both difficult to use
   B. they required miles of wire
   C. they were expensive to operate
   D. they didn't exist overseas

3. When was the telephone invented?
   A. 1840
   B. 1876
   C. 1889
   D. 1896

4. How did Strowger improve the telephone?
   A. He made it wireless.
   B. He trained operators to work them.
   C. He developed a touch-tone system.
   D. He invented a dialing system.

5. Who invented the wireless telegraph?
   A. Almon Strowger
   B. Guglielmo Marconi
   C. Nikola Tesla
   D. Alexander Graham Bell

6. Who invented the radio?
   A. Dr. Martin Cooper
   B. Guglielmo Marconi
   C. Nikola Tesla
   D. Alexander Graham Bell

7. Who used the first mobile car phones?
   A. the police and taxis
   B. Bell and Morse
   C. Dr. Martin Cooper
   D. Internet users

8. The first cellular phone call was made in
   A. 1910
   B. 1927
   C. 1965
   D. 1973

INFERENCE

9. Which of the following statements is true?
   A. All birds can carry messages for people.
   B. Drums are a modern way of signalling.
   C. A flashing light is a visual signal.
   D. Smoke signals are newer than drums.

10. How might people use cell phones in the near future?
   A. to make a sandwich
   B. to plant flowers
   C. to make a bed
   D. to turn on the coffee maker

VOCABULARY REVIEW

WHICH MEANING?

From Chapter 1: *Alexander Graham Bell: Father of the Telephone*

1. What does *close* mean in the following sentence?

> Alexander spoke to his mother in a low tone with his mouth very close to her forehead.

   A. close *(verb)* to stop operation
   B. close *(adjective)* lacking fresh air
   C. close *(adjective)* near

From Chapter 2: *Boston: A City of Firsts*

2. What does *mouth* mean in the following sentence?

> Because it is on a peninsula at the mouth of a river, there was never much room for the city to grow.

   A. mouth *(noun)* the body part through which we take in food
   B. mouth *(noun)* the place where a river empties into the ocean
   C. mouth *(noun)* the opening at the top of a container

From Chapter 3: *Communicating with the World*

3. What does *free* mean in the following sentence?

> He did this so that he could keep one hand free while using the telephone.

   A. free *(adjective)* costing nothing
   B. free *(adjective)* not used
   C. free *(verb)* to let a prisoner go

WRONG WORD

One word in each group does not fit. Circle the word.

1. spectacular	commonplace	fantastic	amazing
2. communication	fiber optics	transmission	marathon
3. understand	decode	patent	translate
4. exchange	incident	trade	replace
5. transmit	patent	innovation	invention
6. ancestor	settler	pioneer	option

WORDS IN CONTEXT

Fill in the blanks with words from each box.

challenged	controversial	fireworks	patriots	vocal chords

1. The city put on a spectacular _____ show this year.
2. The teacher _____ the students to work harder.
3. The new method was very _____. It caused a great deal of disagreement.
4. Many of the _____ of the American Revolution were from Boston.
5. Our _____ move when we speak.

independence	innovation	newsletter	settlement	textiles

6. Many _____ are made of cotton, wool, or silk.
7. The first _____ was north of Boston in Salem.
8. The colonies fought for _____ from England in 1775.
9. I receive a _____ about new technology for teachers every month.
10. Automobiles were an _____ that changed the way of life in the United States.

distance	housed	incident	transmit	visual

11. The police looked into the _____ at the school. Someone had broken a window.
12. A smoke signal is an example of a _____ message.
13. The Declaration of Independence is _____ at the National Archives in Washington, D.C.
14. Please _____ this message immediately.
15. Radio signals can travel over a great _____.

WORD FAMILIES

Fill in the blanks with words from each box.

perfect *(adjective)*	perfect *(verb)*	perfection *(noun)*

1. The inventor spent years trying to achieve _____.
2. Architecture is the _____ career for her. She is a very innovative designer.

settle *(verb)*	settler *(noun)*	settlement *(noun)*

3. The first _____ was near the lake. People could fish and get fresh water.

4. Many immigrants in the 1800s decided to _____ in the Northeast.

transmit *(verb)*	transmitter *(noun)*	transmission *(noun)*

5. The new cell phone tower will help improve _____. The signal has been very weak in our neighborhood.

6. The _____ on our radio has broken. Now we can't pick up any stations.

WRAP IT UP

DISCUSS THE THEME

Read these questions and discuss them with your partner.

1. Do you like to talk on the telephone? Who do you talk with most often? How long do you normally talk?

2. Do you have a cell phone? Do you do other things with this phone except make calls?

3. Do you think that people using cell phones in public are rude? Does your partner agree? Why do you think the way that you do?

RESPOND IN WRITING

Look back at the unit and choose the passage you enjoyed the most. Read it again. Write a one-paragraph summary of the passage in your notebook.

What do you think is the most interesting thing about this passage, and why? Write a paragraph in your notebook.

ESSENTIAL READING SKILLS: ANSWER KEY AND EXPLANATIONS

WHAT TO DO BEFORE YOU READ

A.

1. *Possible answer*: A man with dark hair is posing in front of a scene with fire. The second photo shows a man in several sets of handcuffs.

2. Answers will vary.

3. *Possible answer*: It is an old photograph.

4. *Possible answer*: Maybe the passage will be about magic.

B.

1. The caption on the left tells us that this man's name is David Copperfield. It also has his date of birth. The caption on the right tells us that that this man's name is Harry Houdini. It has the dates when he was born and when he died.

2. The man on the left is still living. The man on the right is no longer living. The first date is the year of birth; the second date is the year of death.

3. Answers will vary.

C.

1. The title mentions tricks and illusions, so the passage is about a thing.

2. These are people who did magic tricks.

3. *Possible answer*: The subtitles help to organize the information in the passage. Each section is about a different trick.

4. The first paragraph is the introduction.

5. The last paragraph is the conclusion.

6. *Possible answer*: The passage will be about magic and illusions.

D.

1. These are key vocabulary words.

2. Italics are used for more than one purpose. In the passage, italics are used for the name of a newspaper. They are also used to show a word.

WHAT TO DO WHILE YOU READ

A.

1. It's nonfiction. It has subtitles. It has the names of real people and places as well as dates. It also has some technical words.

2. Cut and Restore Rope Trick

B.

1. **float**
2. *The London Mirror*
3. 1874
4. three
5. Egypt
6. Bess
7. elephant

C.

True. The passage says that Siegfried and Roy made an elephant disappear. (see line 82)

> **TIP:** Remember to decide what type of information to look for.

D.

1. What is the main topic of the passage?

   A is not correct. This is an example of a type of illusion.

   B is not correct. The passage mentions some famous magicians but not the first one.

   C is the correct answer.

   D is not correct. The passage only briefly mentions ancient Egypt.

E.

2. The cups and balls trick

   A is not correct. This is one of the correct answers, but **B** and **C** are also correct.

   B is not correct. This is one of the correct answers, but **A** and **C** are also correct.

   C is not correct. This is one of the correct answers, but **A** and **B** are also correct.

   D is correct. This is the correct answer. It includes the information in **A**, **B**, and **C**.

TIP: Don't choose the first answer that is correct. Read all of the choices.

3. Which of the following is needed for the cups and balls trick?

   A is the correct answer. A person needs quick, or fast, hands for this trick.

   B is not correct. A television camera is not needed.

   C is not correct. The passage does not mention a trunk with this trick.

   D is not correct. Only **A** is a correct answer.

TIP: Don't assume that "all of the above" is the correct answer. Read all of the choices.

4. When the magician shuffles cards, what happens?

   A is not correct. A trunk is not mentioned.

   B is the correct answer. When you shuffle cards, you mix them.

   C is not correct. The cards are not cut in half.

   D is not correct. The cards are not put in a cup.

TIP: Eliminate any choices that you know are clearly wrong.

5. For the rope trick, the rope is in the magician's

   A is not correct. A coat is not mentioned.

   B is not correct. A hat is not mentioned.

   C is the correct answer. The rope is in the magician's palm. The palm is a part of the hand.

   D is not correct. Handcuffs are not mentioned.

TIP: Remember to think about synonyms.

6. Which word below means the same as *change*?

   A is not correct. *Publicity* means "information about someone in the news."

   B is not correct. *Location* means "place."

   C is not correct. *Audience* means "people watching a performance."

   D is correct.

TIP: Look for definitions in context.

7. Houdini was an expert at

   A is not correct. Animals are not mentioned with Houdini.

   B is not correct. Making large objects disappear is not mentioned with Houdini.

   C is not correct. Card tricks are not mentioned with Houdini.

   D is correct. The passage mentions that Houdini was a great escape artist.

TIP: Sometimes you need to look at details from different places in the passage.

8. Many people consider Houdini

   A is not correct. He was a trapeze artist when he was 9 years old, but he probably wasn't the best in the world.

   B is not correct. The passage mentions that magicians have been around for a long time.

   C is correct. The passage says that Houdini was perhaps the greatest illusionist and escape artist of all time.

   D is not correct. Houdini used handcuffs, but he was not a criminal.

TIP: Be careful of superlatives.

F.

9. Which of the following is **not** true?

   A is the correct answer. Copperfield did not move the Statue of Liberty, so he did not damage it.

   B is not the correct answer. His assistants turned on and off the lights, so they helped him trick the audience.

   C is not the correct answer. The television cameras were used to trick the audience.

   D is not the correct answer. Turning on and off the lights played an important part in the illusion.

> **TIP: Be careful of words like _not_.**

10. What can we say about Siegfried and Roy?

   A is not correct. Although they could have used television cameras, there is nothing in the passage to suggest that they did.

   B is not correct. Nothing in the passage suggests that they made large objects other than elephants disappear.

   C is not correct. The elephant was well trained, but there is no reason to assume that an elephant could escape from handcuffs.

   D is correct. Roy rode the elephant, and it walked out of a door in the box, so we can assume that they may also have trained the animal.

> **TIP: Be careful of inappropriate inferences.**

G.

1. **B** Houdini was able to **manipulate** the key <u>with his hands</u> and even <u>with his teeth</u>.

2. **A** For other tricks, magicians cut people in half or make objects and people **float** <u>through the air</u>.

3. **C** Houdini became even more famous as a result of this trick and the **publicity** that _The London Mirror_ gave him. The <u>newspaper published</u> <u>many stories</u> about the handcuff escape.

4. This trick uses handcuffs, <u>the metal device that police use to hold a</u> <u>prisoner's hands</u>.

5. Master illusionists like <u>David Copperfield</u> can make the Statue of Liberty in New York City disappear.

6. Houdini stood on top of the trunk while a curtain <u>concealed</u>, or <u>hid</u>, his entire body.

7. The trunk had a hidden panel, and the assistant could get out through that <u>small secret door</u>.

8. The word _metamorphosis_ means "<u>a change</u>."

VOCABULARY INDEX